CW01663022

HELLO HAPPY!

A teenager's guide to creating positive mental health

Copyright © 2021 Eleanor Hatherley

All rights reserved. No part of this publication may be reproduced, distributed, or transmitted in any form or by any means, including photocopying, recording, or other electronic or mechanical methods, without the prior written permission of the author, except in the case of brief quotations embodied in critical reviews and certain other non-commercial uses permitted by copyright law.

First edition 2021

ISBN 978-1-8382109-1-5

The content of this book is for informational purposes only. It is not meant to be used, nor should it be used, to diagnose, treat, cure, or prevent any physical or psychological condition or disease. It is not intended as a substitute for consultation with a licensed physician or healthcare practitioner. Consult with your own doctor or mental healthcare practitioner to ensure the information contained in this book will not harm you. I am not liable for any damages or negative consequences arising out of or in connection with the use of this book. Reading this book implies your acceptance of this disclaimer.

Design: Eleanor Hatherley
Illustrations: Georgia Light
Doodles: Eden Hatherley

www.eleanorhatherley.com
@hellohappyteen

This book is dedicated to Lily and Dixie

THANKS TO...

Eden for all the interesting conversations we have shared. Your wisdom and perception is always amazing and it has been a privilege to watch you blossom.

Simon for your unwavering love and support and for modelling how truly being yourself at all times brings you an abundance of happiness, confidence and success.

Roger, Priscilla, Hannah, Clare and Becky for all the love, fun, wisdom and adventures over the years. I couldn't ask for a more interesting family.

CONTENTS

Ask your parents to read this if you are under 18

NOTE TO PARENTS

It can be uncomfortable for young people to share their deepest thoughts and feelings with their parents, so I have created this book as a self-help guide for teenagers.

It will help them to uncover and change the root cause of any poor mental health so that they can start to feel happier. They will also learn a simple tool which will enable them to manage their emotions better.

It would be good for them to work through the book on their own as much as possible. However, it may be useful if you were to offer your support should they need it.

If your child is struggling with a really big mental health issue or has recently experienced a trauma, the book may bring up strong emotions for them. This is a good thing but they may need the support of an appropriate adult to prevent them feeling overwhelmed. In this case I would advise that you work with them and help them with the exercises, or find a suitable professional to support them (see the Resources section of my website for a list of recommended therapies).

Please note that this book contains opinions and observations based on my own experiences and learnings and is not a substitute in any way for a medical or psychological diagnosis or for treatment by a qualified practitioner. You must seek professional help for your teenager where appropriate. I am not responsible or liable for the reactions or the subsequent actions of anyone reading this book.

INTRODUCTION

I have written this book for ALL teenagers, whatever the state of your mental health.

Perhaps you just want to feel a bit happier and more confident, or you need to get on top of something like anxiety or depression, or you have a overwhelming condition that has taken you over.

I am a therapist (and a mum) and I am going to help you to understand how you can create really good mental health. I am not going to focus on managing symptoms as there are plenty of books that already do that. Instead we are going to dive in deep and work out what is at the root of your poor mental health so that you can change it PERMANENTLY.

For some of you, going deep will seem like a good thing and for others it might feel a bit scary or overwhelming. However you feel, I promise that I'm going to make it all as clear and straightforward as possible and that I will guide you safely and carefully through any difficult bits.

This book is quite long. If you don't like reading, just read one chapter each day. Make a commitment to reading the whole book though as there is a lot of useful stuff including exercises to help you uncover your patterns, a self-help tool for managing emotions and a personalised action plan.

If your mental health is very poor and you struggle with your emotions, I recommend that you get some support from an appropriate adult while working through the book.

Your story

So what's your story? Are you happy? Do you feel confident and relaxed in your own skin? Is life an exciting adventure, full of endless possibilities?

I'm betting that the answer is probably NO. Even if you generally feel okay, happiness might be far down on your list. Instead perhaps you are struggling with stuff like anxiety, overwhelm or depression. Or maybe you find it difficult to cope with your emotions, or your confidence and self-belief are rock bottom. Some of you might even feel as if you are clinging onto your sanity with your fingertips some days.

You are not alone. The following is a list of mental health issues that teenagers commonly suffer from:

- Anxiety
- Stress
- Panic attacks
- Phobias
- OCD
- Depression
- Nervous breakdowns
- Hearing voices
- Suicidal thoughts
- Self harm
- Anorexia, bulimia and other eating disorders
- Body dysmorphia
- Identity, gender or sexuality issues
- Struggling with autism, Aspergers and other syndromes
- Feeling overwhelmed
- Negative thoughts
- Lack of confidence
- Self hatred
- Insecurity about your looks, body, personality, abilities or behaviour
- Feeling like you don't fit in or that you are different or weird
- Feeling unloved or unlovable
- Bullying issues
- Problems with parents, siblings, friends or relationships
- Exam pressure

Although these issues are very common, it doesn't make it any easier to deal with them. You are at an age where you don't always want to share your deepest emotions with your parents and, even if you do, they don't always know how to help you. This can leave you feeling out of control, unhappy, scared, ashamed and really down on yourself.

Creating symptoms

So what can you do to feel better? How can you create really positive mental health so that you can start to feel happy again?

As I've already said, we are going to dive in deep in this book. I'm going to start this process by telling you something very important:

➤ ***We create our own mental health.***

You might find this difficult or uncomfortable to accept. Perhaps you are more comfortable with the idea that this stuff just HAPPENS to you and you are an innocent victim. But mental health issues are not things that just randomly happen, they are symptoms of our own deepest innermost subconscious thoughts, beliefs and perceptions about ourselves, other people and the world.

The word 'subconscious' is important here. Our minds are divided into two parts – the subconscious and the conscious. The subconscious mind is like a powerful computer programme running in the background. This means that we are not really aware of it and don't have much control over it. And it's THIS part of your mind that is responsible for creating your mental health problem. This means that you are not CONSCIOUSLY creating it, so don't beat yourself up.

I also wanted to add a quick disclaimer. We don't fully know what causes some of the more serious mental health issues and there may well be cases where there is a chemical, neurological or structural cause. Even then, though, I would still bet that your subconscious thoughts, beliefs and perceptions are definitely adding to the problem. Also, the physical body is very responsive to your thoughts so I'm going to throw in the idea that perhaps your thoughts and perceptions might be causing or adding to some of these chemical, neurological or structural problems?

Time to change

Let's assume that we can ALL benefit from looking at and changing our inner world.

Whether you are comfortable or not with the idea that you might be creating your own mental health, by the end of this book you will understand exactly how and why this is happening and how you can make deep and lasting changes so that you create happiness instead.

So, the big question is:

➤ ***Why do some people's subconscious thoughts, beliefs and perceptions create happiness, confidence and relaxation while other people's create stuff like anxiety, depression or other mental health issues?***

We will be exploring this in depth and by the time you have finished this book you will see yourself, and others, in a totally different light!

So, right now, just for a moment, take a deep breath and let go of all your problems, fears and issues. Open your mind to knowing that there is an amazing and happy version of yourself waiting to be rediscovered. And I am going to show you how to do this.

Let's make a start. First we are going to look at four things that I believe are at the core of poor mental health:

1. Trying to be like everyone else.
2. Creating an untrue story about yourself.
3. Not loving (or even liking) yourself.
4. Traumatic events and inherited patterns.

We will explore each of these in turn in the next section.

SECTION 1

Four reasons why we get poor mental health

CHAPTER 1

Trying to be like everyone else

The first thing that leads us into poor mental health is trying to be like everyone else, rather than just being yourself.

Each person makes up part of a whole and for a successful society we need people with every trait – strong, fast, patient, cheerful, serious, fun, deep thinking, clever, solid, creative, caring, tough, kind, sensitive, nurturing, driven, bossy, organised, chaotic, and so on.

Rather than everyone having all these traits, it makes sense that we all have different traits so we can really make them our thing. If you think of the adults you know, you will see that they are all very different.

Although some traits may seem more attractive than others, actually they are all just as important. So that means if you are shy and caring then you are just as important to the group as someone who is confident and funny.

→ ***Think of it like a jigsaw puzzle. Some people are the details in the foreground, while quite a lot of us are buildings or sky or trees or water. But if you took any one piece out it would spoil the picture equally.***

Pressure from society

The problem is that in our society there's this kind of IDEAL person that we feel we should be – clever, hard working, confident, likeable, funny, fun, interesting, attractive, successful, reliable, organised, honest, kind. Because these kind of traits are so valued, we think there is something wrong with us if we are not like this.

We are also bombarded with images of successful celebrities with exciting lives, beautiful models and aspirational advertising. Social media doesn't help either as it makes it look as if everyone else is popular, happy and sexy.

A lot of SHOULDS start to come in – we should look a certain way, act in a certain way, be able to do certain things. We start to judge ourselves if we are not like this. Perhaps we are not enough (too quiet, not clever enough, not attractive enough) or perhaps we are too much (too loud, emotional, annoying, chaotic, big, clumsy). We start focusing on our faults and where we think we are wrong, rather than seeing who we REALLY are.

Focusing on your gifts

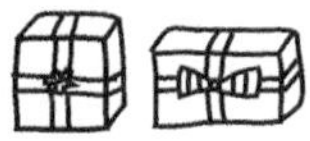

We are ALL born with a unique personality and we all have our own qualities. Sometimes these are not obvious to us as we don't tend to notice the things we are naturally good at. It's always easier to focus on what we are not good at and where we think we are defective.

➤ ***If you can't find anything to feel good about then this is a sign that you have been focusing on your faults. Ask a friend or a parent to tell you something that's great about you. Other people will be able to see your good points much more clearly.***

Your special qualities don't need to be really big and amazing. They could be something that seems very small, like being really calm, or being kind to animals, or being very organised. One of my friends is always really happy and everywhere she goes she makes other people feel happy as her happiness is infectious. What a lovely but simple gift to have.

You might be reasonably good at everything but not amazing at anything. That's great – we need lots of people like that to hold things together. These are often the people who work quietly in the background providing essential support for others, keeping everything ticking over. You are just as necessary as people with big personalities or inspiring talents.

Being yourself at school

When you are young, you spend a lot of time in classrooms at school. It can be hard to be fully yourself as you have to fit in and follow rules and most of the day is spent sitting still and using your brain to concentrate. It's easy to see yourself as a failure if you are not good at these things.

Some traits definitely work better for us at school. For example, if you are good, quiet, tidy, organised, clever and you have a good memory then you will probably find it easy. If you are loud, chaotic, opinionated, bossy, energetic and creative then you will find school much harder – but you'll make a great boss one day (perhaps even of your own company).

➤ ***There are many different sorts of intelligence and only a few of them are tested at school. Perhaps you are good with children or animals, or you can think creatively outside the box, or you are good at leading? Don't write yourself off just because you aren't good at writing essays and sitting exams.***

Another big part of school is the social side. If you are a teenager, especially age 11 to 16, it will feel really important to be liked and accepted by your peer group. This is because you are going through a development stage where you are starting to emotionally detach from the safety of your family group. As your sense of identity as an individual isn't very strong yet, you look for a new group to belong to. Fitting in with this group is more of a priority than being yourself.

But as time goes on everyone will start to find their own identity and your peer group will become less important. By the time you reach your late teens you will be enjoying your own uniqueness and you will also start to gain more control over your life, choosing what you do and who you spend your time with.

So, if you are struggling to fit in with your peer group, stand back and look at the bigger picture. Ultimately the route to being a happy adult lies in finding your own identity and your own community (friends, partners etc) and this will start to happen once you leave school.

Feeling like you are too different

Quite a few teenagers feel like they are just TOO different. Perhaps you have an unusual and quirky personality, or perhaps you have something like autism, Aspergers or ADHD which means your brain is wired a little differently. You may feel as if it is hard to fit in, or that your social skills aren't very good, or that you can't do some of the stuff that others can do. This can make you feel scared that you aren't going to cope with the world. It can also make you really give up on yourself, as if you are defective in some way.

But the fact that you are different is a really good thing. You are designed to be different. You will have the potential to bring difference to society in the future – perhaps through creativity or innovation or just by putting a different slant on things.

The main thing is not to focus on needing to be the same as everyone else. Doing this will stop you feeling comfortable with your differences. Focus on what you CAN do rather than what you CAN'T do and you'll start to appreciate yourself much more.

➤ ***A great example is Anne Hegerty from the TV show,*** **I'm A Celebrity.** ***She has Aspergers and had a difficult childhood with no friends. She also struggled as a young adult, almost becoming homeless before she found high level quizzing. Her amazing memory for facts led to a job on*** **The Chase** ***and then on to*** **I'm A Celebrity.** ***In addition, while on*** **I'm A Celebrity,** ***she talked openly about her Aspergers. This in turn created more awareness about it and helped other people to deal with their own feelings about it. So she has also contributed to society in a meaningful and helpful way as well as creating a financially successful life for herself.***

I'd just like to point out that you don't have to be a rich celebrity to have a fulfilling and successful life! There are many other ways that you can bring your gifts to the world, whatever they are. Just don't give up on yourself.

Complete Exercise 1 to help you find out who you REALLY are.

EXERCISE 1 Who are you?

Write down some things that you like about yourself or that you are good at. If you find this hard, ask a friend or a parent for some ideas.

Now write down some things that you DON'T like about yourself. Spend a few moments really feeling how each of these make you feel, allowing any emotions to come up. Just be with the feelings, don't judge them.

Now see if you can find a way of turning these traits that you don't like about yourself into a positive. Then find a situation where it might be useful (ie "Being sensitive helps me to understand how other people feel so I am good at helping friends").

Get a piece of paper and write your name at the top. Then write down all your traits. Give the traits you don't like a positive angle, ie if you think you are too different, write 'unusual' or, if you think you are shy, write 'sensitive and gentle'. Make it a list to be proud of. Keep adding to the list every time you notice any more traits.

Follow the ongoing actions below as this will help you to understand yourself better.

Ongoing actions

- → Start looking for and focusing on your strengths and your differences. Notice when you are naturally good at something. What makes you different? What do people like about you? Look for small things as well as big things.
- → Look at your list of traits every day to help you get in touch with who you really are.
- → Notice when you are focusing on where you think you are lacking and when you are trying to be like everyone else.

CHAPTER 2

Creating an untrue story about yourself

The second thing that can create poor mental health is the story we create about ourselves and the world. If this is negative and untrue then we are always going to be unhappy.

When we are very young children, we love and accept ourselves fully and unconditionally without any judgements. We are happy just to be alive. But then we are gradually 'moulded' by the opinions and expectations of the people around us (parents, siblings, teachers, friends), as well as by our life experiences and the society we live in.

And so we begin to create a story of who we are – our strengths, our weaknesses, how loveable we are, how safe we are, how we should behave, what is wrong with us, and so on. After a while we totally believe this story and we think this is who we are.

If your story of who you are is very negative then this will make you feel very unhappy and stressed.

Being moulded

So how and why does this 'moulding' process happen?

When we are very young, we have no perspective. Our brains are like sponges and we accept everything and don't question it. We believe everything people say about us and we form our opinion of the world and of other people based on our childhood experiences. We also form opinions about ourselves based on what we THINK other people think of us.

➤ ***Oliver's parents were always very strict with him. Because of this he decided that people would only love him when he was being good and getting everything right. Actually the truth was that his parents were just trying to help him be the very best person he could be so that he would be happy and have a really good life.***

Our childhood experiences often lead us to decide that we are defective in some way – that we are less lovable, less powerful, less important than others. This gives us a negative view of ourselves and we reject parts of ourselves as being unacceptable.

So you can see how the people around you and your experiences will literally help to shape you. And if you are a sensitive person this will happen even more as you will be more open and receptive to other people and their expectations and judgements.

Parental influences

Our parents usually have the biggest influence on us. Here are some examples of different types of parenting. Do any of them feel true for you? (Quick note: Some of you will be being raised by other caregivers such as grandparents, step parents or foster parents. I will be using the word 'parents' throughout the book but this will mean ALL caregivers).

- Parents who are very focused on your behaviour and it feels as if they only love you when you are being a certain way (ie good, quiet, helpful, successful).
- Parents who are very domineering and controlling and who try and mould you so much that you end up feeling unconfident and unsure of who you really are.

- Parents who want you to do really well in life which makes you feels as if they only love you when you have achieved something.
- Parents who do love you but find some of your traits or behaviours difficult which makes you feel like there is something wrong with those traits, and therefore with parts of you.
- Parents who are strict, angry or unpredictable which makes you feel scared and unloved.
- Parents who are very busy or caught up in their own stuff so they don't notice you enough and it feels as if you aren't very important.
- Parents who are struggling with their own mental health problems or addictions so you feel alone and unsupported.
- Parents who just don't get you so you feel as if there's something wrong with you.
- Parents who give one or more of your siblings more attention so you feel as if you aren't as loveable or important.
- A parent who leaves the family and is then unreliable about seeing you so that you feel as if you've been rejected and are unlovable.
- Parents who love you so much and make you feel so special that when you go out into the world you feel as if something is wrong with you as no one else seems to like you as much.

If you have identified your parents from this list, think about how that kind of parenting might have moulded you. What might you have decided about yourself as a result of this?

I'd just like to say, this is not about blame. Your parents will be doing the best job they can but they will be driven by their own personalities and issues.

Sisters and brothers

Our relationship with our sisters and brothers can also really affect us. We spend a lot of time with them so they are a big influence. Here are a few examples:

- Siblings who you think are better than you (ie, cleverer, prettier, stronger, more popular, more 'normal'). This makes you feel as if you are not as good as them and are therefore a failure.
- Siblings who seem to get more love and attention than you do which makes you feel as if you are not as loveable.
- Siblings who put you down all the time or don't pay you any attention so you feel useless or not liked. This is often the pattern with an older sibling.

Again, it isn't about blame. Your siblings are just people muddling along in life with their own set of insecurities.

School influences

By the time we go to school we have already started to form a story about who we are, based on our relationship with our parents and our siblings. And then we 'learn' even more about ourselves from other children and from teachers. We might discover that we are louder, or shyer, or not as clever or as popular as everyone else. Because we are so young and don't have any perspective, we see this as a problem and so we judge and reject ourselves even more.

What did you decide about yourself at school?

Being realistic

Many things that you notice about yourself both at home and at school may well have some truth to them. Because we are all different there will be people who ARE cleverer, more attractive, funnier etc than you. The key thing is to accept this and to be okay with how you are. This is very difficult to do as a young child as we don't have any perspective, but can you look at yourself now and see that you ARE different but that you are still lovable and as important and valuable as everyone else?

Let's complete Exercise 2 to help you understand the story you've created about yourself.

EXERCISE 2 What is YOUR story?

What is your relationship like with your parents? How do they treat you? How do they make you feel? What would you change?

Now think about your siblings (if you have any). Do you get on well or do you argue a lot? Or perhaps they just ignore you? How does your relationship with your siblings make you feel?

What was your primary school experience like? Were you happy or did it make you feel unhappy, scared, lonely or different?

Write down all the decisions you have made about yourself based on your relationship with your parents and siblings and on your school experiences (for example, "I'm only lovable when I'm good", or "I'm louder than most other people")?

Read through what you have written a few times and just allow any emotions to come up. You might feel sadness or anger. Don't try and change your feelings or resist them, just welcome them.

Now imagine that you had perfect parents, perfect siblings and a perfect school experience. What story would you have about yourself now? Write down a new story of who you are and how life is. You can also bring in any learnings about who you are from Exercise 1. Read it through a few times and really try and feel it.

Follow the ongoing actions below to help you change your story.

Ongoing actions

- Start noticing the stories that you have created about yourself. Are they really true? Is there a bigger picture? How are they affecting your life?
- Read your new story about yourself as often as possible.

CHAPTER 3

Not loving (or even liking) yourself

The third thing that can create mental health issues is not loving ourselves.

I know it'll be a big jump for many of you to love yourself. You are probably struggling with even LIKING yourself a lot of the time. So if you find 'love' a bit too much then just insert the work 'like' for now.

But whether you believe it or not, we are all equally loveable. Imagine a room full of newborn babies. Would you say some of them are less loveable than others? No, they are all perfect beings – and so are you.

If you are struggling to love yourself, look back over the last two chapters. It usually comes from not accepting yourself, focusing on where you think you lack and creating untrue and negative stories about yourself. If you can change this then it will help you to love yourself more.

How loving yourself improves your life

Really loving yourself is probably the MOST IMPORTANT thing you'll ever do in your whole life. The more you love yourself the better your life will be. Here are some reasons why:

- **Loving ourselves means that we have compassion and kindness for ourselves.** We are more accepting of who we are and we focus on our gifts rather than our limitations. We won't compare ourselves with others or try and be something we are not.
- **When things go wrong we are not so hard on ourself.** If we fail at something, we tend to pick ourselves up and try again. We don't give up on ourselves. We don't beat ourselves up for making mistakes, we learn from them.
- **When we love ourselves we cope better with life.** We feel more powerful and more able and we know we can cope with whatever life throws at us.
- **If someone is unkind then it doesn't affect us as much if we love ourself.** Other people's opinions become less important than our own. We don't need to rely on others in order to feel good about ourselves because it comes from within us.
- **When we love ourselves we tend to make better choices.** We don't settle for the first friend or boyfriend/girlfriend that comes along, or the first job. We respect ourselves and make sure we get the best that life can offer.
- **The way we feel about ourselves tends to affect how others feel about us.** Think about the popular people at school. Does it feel as if they like themselves? Are they comfortable with who they are? Are they perfect? No, probably not, but that doesn't bother them. Then think about the less popular people. How much do they like themselves?
- **Our relationship with ourself tends to set the tone for every other relationship we will have.** If we really love ourself then it will be much easier to form healthy and loving relationships with other people.

Can you think of any other ways that loving yourself would make your life better?

Being a good friend

Think of it like a relationship with yourself. What sort of a friend are you to yourself? Are you hard on yourself or are you kind and caring? If you are hard on yourself, did you learn this way of behaving from someone else (perhaps a parent)? What is stopping you being kind and caring?

We have a constant internal conversation with ourselves. Stop and see if you can hear this running in yourself. It's like a little voice in your head. The voice might be critical and negative. Imagine having someone hanging around you all day moaning at you and criticising you. How would that make you feel? And how about if you had a kind and caring person with you who was always on your side. Wouldn't that make you feel happier?

➤ ***Try and be aware of how you treat yourself and the kind of things you are saying to yourself and thinking about yourself. You might be surprised at how negative it is.***

Loving yourself more

It can be difficult to really love yourself, especially if you have been down on yourself for a long time. I am hoping that as you read this book you will start to feel more accepting and kinder towards yourself. It can be a bit of a journey and can take a bit of time though.

We are generally not taught how to love ourselves, often because our parents have not been taught to love themselves either by their parents. The emphasis is more on being polite and kind to others and it can be seen as selfish to put ourselves first. But, as I've already said, our relationship with ourselves sets the tone for our relationships with other people so the more we like and connect with ourselves the more we will like and connect with others.

It's actually useful to do it the other way round too. If you focus on liking and connecting with others (this includes your family, your friends, your pets, other teenagers at school, teachers, celebrities, people in shops, etc) then this will help you to learn to like yourself more. It's almost like you are practising creating a new filter for how you see things and this will gradually extend to how you see yourself. If you are always moaning and bitching and getting angry with other people then you will probably be interacting with yourself in the same way. Try being really kind and loving to everyone for a day and see how it makes you feel.

Here are a few other ideas to help you love yourself more:

- Know that it's hard being a human and you are doing your very best.
- Focus on your gifts rather than your lack.
- Stop comparing yourself with others.
- Let go of any untrue stories you have created about yourself.
- Stop caring what other people think so much and focus on pleasing yourself instead.
- Don't try and be perfect, it's completely normal to fail sometimes.
- Stop looking for love from other people and look for it within yourself.
- Forgive yourself for anything you think you might have done wrong.
- Stop being hard on yourself and be kind to yourself instead.
- Remember that there is so much more to you than how you look.
- Look after your body by eating well, having exercise and getting good sleep.
- Don't hold onto the past but see every day as a new blank canvas.

Some of these may be difficult to do. Perhaps start by picking three that seem relatively easy and practice doing them. Once you have mastered those ones, choose another three, and so on.

Now let's have a look at how you feel about yourself by completing Exercise 3.

EXERCISE 3 Do you like yourself?

Stand a comfortable distance in front of a mirror (a full length one if you have one) and have a good long look at yourself. Rate yourself out of ten for how much you like yourself (0 = I hate myself and 10 = I love myself). Be really honest with yourself, there's no right answer and no one else will know your score. Base it not just on how you look but on your whole self.

Move a bit closer and look into your own eyes. How does this feel? Do any feelings and emotions come up? If so, stay with these feelings for a few moments without judging them, even if they are negative or uncomfortable. Just allow yourself to really feel them.

Now smile at yourself and say "Hi", as if you are meeting someone new. Allow yourself to feel kindness towards yourself, like you would towards a pet or someone else you love. Don't worry if it feels hard.

If this exercise feels uncomfortable, then practise doing it every day. Allow any feelings to come up and practice connecting kindly with yourself.

Follow the ongoing actions below so that you can start to improve your relationship with yourself.

Ongoing actions

- Make a list of reasons why you don't love yourself and then look at each reason and ask yourself if it is really true.
- Look out for the little voice inside your head. Notice what it's saying. Is it generally positive or negative? If you notice it being negative, tell yourself something positive and kind instead.
- Notice when you are focusing on your lack rather than your gifts. Also look out for any untrue stories that you might have created.

CHAPTER 4

Trauma and inherited patterns

The fourth thing that can create mental health issues is trauma and inherited patterns. Let's look at each of these.

What is trauma?

When we experience something that is very overwhelming and frightening that we find difficult to cope with, it is known as A TRAUMA.

Generally there are two types of traumas:

1. **Sudden one-off shocks.** These are things that happen to us that suddenly overwhelm us. They can range from really big things like someone dying, being in an accident, having major surgery, down to smaller things like losing your parent in the supermarket when you are very young, or being told off unexpectedly.
2. **Ongoing traumas.** We can also experience ongoing traumas that happen over and over again. Examples might be having an angry and unpredictable parent who shouts a lot, being abused, being bullied at school, or a sibling constantly being mean to you.

Most of us have probably experienced both of these types of traumas.

Traumas can range from massive, right down to really small. If the trauma is massive, it can really affect us. It might show up later as something like addiction, OCD, an eating disorder, outbursts of strong emotion, not being able to form relationships or hold jobs down, or severe anxiety and depression.

If the trauma is small it won't necessarily cause such a problem outwardly but it can still cause subtle changes in how you see yourself and the world and could still have quite a big impact in the long run.

➤ ***So what determines whether a trauma is big or small?***

The interesting thing is that it isn't really about what happened, it's about how you feel about it. Now I know that some traumas are bigger than others and there is certainly some obvious relationship between the size of the trauma and the size of the reaction, but we do all react differently to the same outside events.

Let's take the scenario of what seems like something quite small – being shouted at by a parent when you are young. Here are four typical reactions that might happen:

1. You might enjoy getting attention from the parent.
2. You might feel a bit upset but know your parent was right so you are not too bothered.
3. You might feel shocked, upset and angry for a few days and change your behaviour so that it doesn't ever happen again.
4. You might feel so shocked and overwhelmed that you start suffering from anxiety and constantly avoid any situation that might be similar.

Out of these four reactions, only the last two reactions could be categorised as a trauma – the third one is perhaps a mild trauma and the fourth one is a big trauma.

There will be all sorts of factors behind how different people react to traumas, including things like how sensitive they are, how powerful they feel, whether it has happened before, their view of themselves and the world, etc.

Why do traumas create a problem?

We experience traumas as overwhelming situations. They land on us suddenly and, because we can't deal with them, we push them down. When we do this it locks chaos and strong emotions into us and disrupts our nervous systems. We will look at how this works later in the book.

When we are older, we are better at processing traumatic events as they happen. We will think repeatedly about what happened and perhaps talk about it too and will eventually find a way of making peace with it. However, when we are very young, we don't have these processing skills and so the traumas often get locked away for life. We often don't even remember the traumas but they sit in our bodies causing disruption.

Traumas also tend to shape how we look at ourselves and the world. As we have no perspective when we are young, we believe everything that happens to us is truth.

So, for example, if you are attacked, you may end up believing stuff like "The world is a dangerous place", or "There must be something wrong with me for that to happen to me" or "No-one's got my back". These beliefs will stay with you forever and you can imagine how much they might affect you.

When we are young, even traumas that seem very small on the surface can affect us deeply and change our perceptions about ourselves. Here is an example of the sort of small trauma that could have a big impact:

➤ ***Tom had to do a presentation at school in front of his class. He stood up but felt so nervous that he went bright red and couldn't speak. The other children laughed and he decided that he was too sensitive and that it wasn't safe to draw attention to himself or speak out ever again.***

The decisions he made will probably affect him for the rest of his life. As an adult, Tom might feel that he is oversensitive and will be unconfident and shy around people. He will keep in the background, avoiding any situation where he stands out. He will definitely be very uncomfortable with any kind of public speaking. Imagine how much all of that will hold him back and stop him living fully – and all just from one small trauma!

As a therapist, I have worked with many adults who are struggling with something in their life and when we look deeper we always uncover at least one of these small childhood traumas, so don't underestimate them. I had a client in his 50s who came to me with a massive and paralysing fear of public speaking. We quickly uncovered an event in his childhood that was a bit like Tom's example above. Once we did some work on clearing this, he was able to go off and give a speech at a big event.

Uncovering your traumas

So are there any past traumas that might be affecting you?

Some of you might have experienced something so big and obvious that you immediately feel stressed when you read this question (if this is the case, please be careful and get some support from a parent or another adult that you feel comfortable with). For others it can be difficult to spot your own traumas.

So think back over your life and see if you can think of any traumas that might have affected you. Did you have any big and obvious things happen to you when you were young? Perhaps your parents got divorced, or you lost someone close to you, or you had a serious illness, or surgery? Or perhaps someone shouted at you or was mean to you unexpectedly?

There might have been some patterns in your family or at school which traumatised you (it's worth revisiting the list in Chapter 2 on types of parents as many of these can cause trauma). Did you always have to be perfect? What was your relationship like with your siblings? Were you bullied at school?

Also, ask yourself if you were happy and carefree one moment and then suddenly everything changed and you started feeling anxious, sad or angry a lot of the time. If the answer is YES then what was it that happened? Perhaps a change of school, loss of a friendship, being told off unfairly, something that someone said? These will give you clues to the trauma.

There isn't much we can do about any of the traumas we have had. They have happened and we can't change them. But what we can do is to is to change our relationship with them now so they don't affect us in the same way in the future. We will look at how to do this later in the book.

Inherited patterns

As well as experiencing traumas, we can also inherit patterns and traits from our parents which can cause problems. This can include things like how intelligent we are, what sort of skills we have, if we are extrovert or introvert, whether we have a sunny nature or are more serious and deep thinking, how sensitive or creative we are, etc.

It's often said that anxiety or depression can be inherited. I think that what we are actually inheriting is how our parents' minds work and therefore how they deal with life. This means that we often end up going down the same route as them with our mental health.

As well as what we inherit from our parents, we will also be shaped by their attitudes and beliefs. Remember, your parents will have had their own traumas too when they were young and this will affect them.

➤ ***Are you like one of your parents in the way that you think? What is their mental health like? Are you heading down the same route? How does your other parent deal with things (or a relative on their side of the family if you only have one parent)? Is it more healthy? Could you learn from their way of doing things?***

If reading this has made you realise that you have inherited a way of thinking that will make you more likely to get a mental health issue, don't worry. Your parent will have their own negative perceptions based on their childhood experiences and these will be a big part of the way they think. You don't have to take these on, they are NOT yours. Perhaps talk to them about their early lives, see if you can work out what is going on for them and why they react to the world in the way they do. This will help you to understand and detach from the way that they think. And continue to work through this book as it will help you change your way of thinking.

Complete Exercise 4 to see if you are being triggered by any traumas.

EXERCISE 4 Is trauma affecting you?

Ask yourself what emotion, feeling or behaviour bothers you most in your life. Perhaps an emotion like anger, sadness or anxiety, or feeling trapped, scared or powerless, or a phobia or obsession.

See if you can get in touch with this feeling now. If you start to feel overwhelmed, stop and do some calming breathing instead. You are perfectly safe but I want to give you more tools before you are ready to deal with strong emotions.

If you feel okay to continue, ask yourself "Have I had this emotion/feeling/behaviour all my life or is it recent?". You can also ask yourself "Where does this come from?" or "When is the first time I felt like this?". Allow the answers to pop into your mind rather than trying to think hard. You might remember an event or it might just be something general like "That's how Mum always made me feel".

If you do find an obvious trauma, make a note of it as it will be a good one to clear later. If you didn't find anything, then just sit with the emotion or feeling for a bit longer, if it feels comfortable to do so.

Once you have finished this exercise, do something calming like some deep breathing or listening to some relaxing music.

Follow the ongoing actions below.

Ongoing actions

- Try and notice any future traumas as they happen. Remember trauma is all about perception. Why is this particular thing that just happened such a problem for you?
- Notice any habits or ways of being you copy from your parents.
- Talk to your parents and grandparents about any big traumas they might have had.

SECTION 2

Beliefs, thoughts and feelings

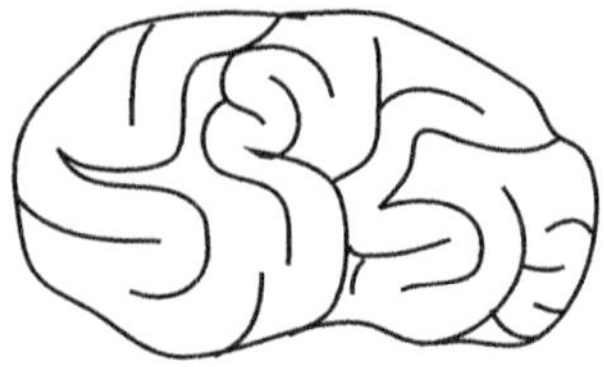

CHAPTER 1

The mind

In the last section we looked at four things that can lead us into poor mental health. Let's quickly summarise them:

1. How we try and be the same as everyone else, a kind of ideal and perfect person, which means that we focus on where we think we are lacking rather than on who we REALLY are.
2. How we can end up creating a negative and untrue story about ourselves based on our experiences, the expectations of the people around us, as well as what we think of ourself and what we think others think of us.
3. How we don't always love or even like ourselves, partly because we are focusing on where we think we lack and partly because of negative stories we have created about ourself.
4. How both traumas and inherited patterns can affect our reactions and our view of ourselves and the world around us.

Although these four things are really important, it can be difficult to change them, even when we know that they are not working for us. In this section we are going to look at how the mind works and this will help you to understand why you think and feel the way you do, and what you can do about it.

Our background wallpaper

We have a fairly constant stream of thoughts going through our minds at all times and these are a mix of negative, neutral and positive. But what determines whether our thoughts are negative, neutral or positive?

Imagine that you have a kind of background 'wallpaper' to all your thoughts. This wallpaper represents your reality about the world. Its pattern and content is determined by your personality, the people around you, your experiences, your learnings and your perceptions.

As you can imagine, the four things listed at the start of this chapter can have a HUGE impact on your wallpaper. If you are not being yourself, are creating untrue stories, not loving yourself and are affected by traumas then your wallpaper has the potential to be very negative. You will then get stuck in a lot of negative thinking and behaviour.

➤ ***Don't beat yourself up if your wallpaper seems very negative. I have never yet met anyone who doesn't have something negative going on in their wallpaper and to be honest most adults have lots of negative stuff.***

The subconscious mind

A lot of the stuff in your wallpaper will be coming from your SUBCONSCIOUS mind. We mentioned the subconscious mind in the introduction. Let's have a look at it in a bit more detail.

The mind is divided into the conscious mind (around 3%) and the subconscious mind (around 97%). The conscious mind is in charge of stuff like logic, reason and making choices. The subconscious mind looks after all the stuff that we do automatically (like walking or writing) and it also contains all our childhood programming.

This programming is mainly laid down during the first seven years of our life when our brain is like a sponge, absorbing everything it comes into contact with. It then runs in the background for the rest of our lives, like a computer programme. This means we are not really aware of it but it will REALLY shape the way we think and behave.

The conscious and subconscious minds work very differently.
The conscious mind can change very quickly but the subconscious mind is more habit based and is therefore hard to change. So, for example, if you read something in this book that gives you an 'aha' moment, your conscious mind would instantly adapt to take the new information in. However, you would need to practice it many times before your subconscious mind started to make any changes.

➛ ***This is probably a good thing. Imagine if we instantly changed our mind every time we read or heard something – we'd be all over the place!***

Although the subconscious mind is slow to change, it is not set in stone and it IS possible to change it. If we want to make deep changes to our mental health, it is very important to get our subconscious mind to work for us rather than against us.

So how do we do this?

Changing the subconscious mind

Your best tool for changing your subconscious mind is actually your conscious mind. If there is something you want to change, try following these four steps:

1. Use the conscious part of your mind to help you work out what you want to change. Perhaps, for example, you need to love yourself more.
2. Then decide what you want instead. How would you like to feel? What would you like to have? Who would you like to be? The subconscious mind likes clear instructions so make the thoughts really clear. Create a picture in your mind of what it will look like and feel like to love yourself more. It doesn't matter if you don't believe it yet – that's your subconscious resisting the change as it is not ready to take the new message on board yet.
3. Then use your conscious mind to focus on this new thought or picture as much as possible. Think of your conscious mind like a SPOTLIGHT. You need to shine that spotlight on this new thought or picture as often as possible.

➛ ***Remember that the subconscious is all about habit and you have to present it with the new thought or picture many times before it will take it on board.***

4. Eventually the new thought or picture will start to get stronger and the old thoughts and pictures will feel less relevant. Think of it like building a new house. You've been living in the old one for years and it's well formed and familiar. You are now building a new and better one next to it. It has to be built brick by brick and, because you are still building it, you won't be living in, just visiting it to build it. But eventually the house will be good enough to move into permanently.

Future positive

Here are some more tips to help you to reprogramme your subconscious mind:

- **Be positive.** Focus on positive things as often as possible. Look for all the good things in your life rather than the bad things. It might take a while to get into the habit of doing this but remember practice, practice, practice as this is how the subconscious is changed.
- **Stop yourself.** Every time you are worrying about something and overthinking, you are actually making all the negative stuff in your subconscious even stronger. Try and notice yourself doing it and then stop and focus on something more positive.
- **Good timing.** It is easier to access your subconscious mind first thing in the morning and last thing at night as you have different brain waves during these times of day. Use this time to focus on new positive messages and to create new images for the future.
- **Persistence.** It takes around 30 days to programme a new thought into your subconscious. So keep going, don't give up easily if it doesn't feel as if it is working.
- **Good influences.** The subconscious is constantly tweaking itself, absorbing new information and creating new beliefs. It is therefore important to feed it good stuff. What are you thinking? What are you

watching, reading and listening to? Stay away from toxic people, avoid social media and other online stuff if it isn't serving you, don't read the news if it depresses or scares you. Instead look for things that make you feel good.

- **Visualise.** The subconscious mind responds well to visualising. Visualising is where we imagine a picture in our mind. Start by asking yourself what you want in life, how you want to feel and what you want to achieve. Then imagine yourself doing these things. Make it as detailed and real as possible. You can either create a still picture or make a little movie. Then focus on it as often as you can – at least 10-15 minutes every day.

  ➛ ***If you think you can't visualise, ask yourself what colour your family car is. You will know straight away and what you will actually have done is to create a picture of the car in your mind.***

- **Hypnosis.** The subconscious responds well to hypnosis as it mimics the state that it was in when it was first programmed. Hypnosis is a type of therapy where you listen to a script which can help you make changes to your subconscious. It's not a quick fix though and you will need to commit to listening to your script every day for at least 30 days. If you don't want to go to a hypnotherapist, you can also find simple free hypnosis scripts online.

Let's have a look at Exercise 5 to practice changing your subconscious.

EXERCISE 5 Changing your subconscious

We could all do with loving ourselves more so let's work on that.

Use your conscious mind to work out why loving yourself might be a problem for you. Get as much information as possible. What has happened to you to make you decide that you are not loveable? Does it come from your relationship with your parents or a sibling? Or perhaps something that has happened with friends or at school?

Now close your eyes and take a few deep breaths. Think how you would feel if you really loved yourself and felt that others loved you too. It might be hard to imagine but do your best. Create a little movie of yourself at home with your family (or with friends if that feels easier). Imagine yourself smiling and happy, feeling really loved by the people around you. Imagine feeling loving towards them and towards yourself. Really get in touch with how it makes you feel. It might bring up some sadness but that is okay, just feel it, it will pass.

Sit for a few moments with this movie. Breathe it into every cell in your body. Make it as real as possible. Really connect with it.

Follow the ongoing actions below to work on your subconscious.

Ongoing actions

- Go back to the above movie as often as possible. Do it when you first wake up and again before you go to sleep. Keep doing it every day for at least a month until you feel more loving towards yourself.
- Keep following the list of tips on the previous two pages so that you can start to make your subconscious work better for you.

CHAPTER 2

Limiting beliefs

One of the main things that is found in your background wallpaper is beliefs about yourself and the world. These come from your subconscious mind and they create your sense of reality.

Many of your beliefs are correct but you will also have formed many that are untrue. These negative and untrue beliefs are known as 'limiting beliefs' and they hold us back from our full potential and prevent us from being happy.

➛ ***The more negative your wallpaper is, the more limiting beliefs you'll have.***

Here are a few examples of limiting beliefs:

- "I'm ugly"
- "I'm not loveable"
- "I'm weak and powerless"
- "I'm too much"
- "I'm all alone"
- "It's not safe to stand out"
- "People are out to get me"

These limiting beliefs really hold you back from being happy and they will also hold you back in friendships, relationships and careers later in your life. We ALL have limiting beliefs, even really happy confident people, but the more negative your background wallpaper is, the more you will have.

Creating limiting beliefs

There are two ways that limiting beliefs are formed:

1. **Limiting beliefs that start gently, like an opinion.** These get more set in stone over time as we look for and find more things that seem to support them.

   For example, if your dad always sides with your sister then you may start to think that he loves her more than he loves you. You will start looking out for things that support this idea until you have enough evidence to form a limiting belief, perhaps something like "I am not as loveable as my sister". Because you are young and don't understand the complexity of things, this is very over simplified and completely untrue. Perhaps your dad is taking your sister's side because she is younger, or can't defend herself very well. Or perhaps your sister is more like your dad so he finds her easier to parent? And even in the rare case that your parent does find your sibling easier to care about, this still doesn't mean you are less loveable. There are MILLIONS of other people in the world, why make that decision about yourself based on just ONE person's opinion!

2. **Limiting beliefs that are formed in the moment when we are in an emotionally overwhelming situation.** This usually happens when we are very young and the subconscious is looking for a way to make sense of a dangerous situation in order to keep us safe. Because of this safety aspect, the subconscious tends to hold on to these type of limiting beliefs very tightly, even when they are not serving us any more.

   An example of this might be when you get told off by a teacher in front of the class for getting your homework wrong. You weren't expecting it and it is a shock. A couple of the other children laugh and you feel completely overwhelmed with emotions such as shame and embarrassment. The emotion is so strong that the subconscious mind makes a decision that the situation is not safe. And so limiting beliefs are formed to prevent it happening again, perhaps something like "I mustn't ever make mistakes". Again, with perspective, we can look back and see that teachers are just human and they do get annoyed sometimes about small things. And the other children only laughed because it was a bit of fun in an otherwise boring lesson.

It's important to realise that your limiting beliefs are NOT facts or truth. They are just conclusions you came to based on what you knew at the time and what felt safe. They may have served you well then but they are probably holding you back now and the sooner you can start to let them go the better.

Finding your limiting beliefs

Hopefully just understanding about limiting beliefs will help you be more aware of some of yours and this can start to loosen and shift them a bit.

The good news is that it's easier to change your limiting beliefs when you are younger as they are less set in stone. Your brain is still forming and is more adaptable than an older adult brain. So now is a really good time to start challenging your beliefs.

Using the list in Box 1, see if you can spot some of your main limiting beliefs. You can tick all the ones that feel true for you and put stars against the ones that seem really relevant.

There will also be lots of clues to your limiting beliefs in your behaviour. For example, when you have negative thoughts, feel scared or anxious, worry about not being or doing things perfectly, or fear failing or making mistakes, there will be at least one negative belief behind it. So, if you are feeling scared, for example, what is it you believe about yourself or the world (ie, "I'm not strong enough", "I am vulnerable", "The world is dangerous", "I am all alone")? Or if you feel as if you can't do something, what do you believe about your abilities (ie, "I am not as clever as others", "It's not okay to fail", "It's not safe to fail")?

BOX 1 Common core limiting beliefs

- I am not good enough
- I am not clever enough
- I am stupid
- I am useless
- I am not enough
- I am not important
- I am unattractive
- I am too fat/thin
- I am ugly
- I am not likeable
- I am not loveable
- I am weird or different
- I am defective
- I am boring
- I am a horrible person
- I am a failure
- I am too sensitive
- I am too emotional
- I am too much
- I am too loud
- Parts of me aren't acceptable
- People aren't interested in me
- What I have to say is not important
- People must like me
- I have to do things perfectly
- I must not make mistakes
- I must not fail
- I have to please people
- I must not create conflict
- Conflict is not safe
- I won't be able to cope
- I am weak
- I am vulnerable
- I am powerless
- I will never get what I want
- Change is difficult
- Life is difficult
- I am not safe
- The world is not safe
- I am not safe in my body
- I am going to die
- My body is going to fail
- Something's going to get me
- Life is against me
- Other people are dangerous
- People are against me
- I must not stand out
- I have to be in control
- Life is overwhelming
- I am all alone
- There is no one to support me
- No-one's got my back

➛ ***Whenever you are feeling bad, see if you can spot the limiting beliefs that might be affecting you. Write these down. You will soon start to notice which ones are the real troublemakers for you.***

Changing your limiting beliefs

When you have identified some of your limiting beliefs, you can start to challenge them by asking yourself these six questions:

1. **When and why was this belief formed?** You might know the answer straight away or you might just have a general feeling about it. Perhaps it was a decision you made about yourself based on something someone said, or perhaps you had a trauma and you were emotionally overwhelmed? Or have you learnt it from a parent?
2. **What do you know now that you didn't know then?** As most limiting beliefs are formed before the age of seven, we don't have much perspective and see things in a very simplistic and often totally incorrect way. Stand back and look at the belief with more grown up eyes.
3. **Is the belief really true?** Your immediate reaction might be 'yes' because you are so used to having it. But is it really true, deep down? Are you just creating it by constantly looking out for evidence of it? Would other people agree that it was true? Is it true all the time, or perhaps just occasionally? Perhaps it might have felt true once but does it have to be true for the rest of your life?
4. **Is this belief serving you?** We form beliefs to keep ourselves safe – and it probably worked well at the time. But is it still working for you? Perhaps it's time to let it go?
5. **What is the opposite of the belief?** For example, if you feel weak and powerless, say "I am powerful", "I am strong". These are called positive affirmations. If you find your mind arguing ("No, I'm NOT strong"), then say "I am power", "I am strength" instead. This helps you to connect with a kind of universal source of power and strength rather than just your own which may feel limited. I have called these 'universal affirmations' and there is a list of them in Box 2.

BOX 2 Universal affirmations

- I am strength
- I am courage
- I am happiness
- I am confidence
- I am positivity
- I am beauty
- I am power
- I am perfection
- I am love
- I am connection
- I am joy
- I am invincibility
- I am resilience
- I am physical perfection
- I am health
- I am persistence
- I am safety
- I am trust
- I am acceptance
- I am forgiveness
- I am gratitude
- I am stillness
- I am peace
- I am relaxation

6. **How would my life improve without this belief?** What could you could be, do, have and feel if you didn't have this limiting belief? What would your future look like without it?

Changing your beliefs can take persistence, time and practice. Remember that they come from the subconscious mind and that the only way to make changes at this level is through repeating something over and over again for at least 30 days.

You may also find that some of your really core limiting beliefs are hard to shift as they are woven into complicated subconscious thought structures. But just keep working on them. If you even just shift the intensity of the beliefs a bit then that will help you to feel better.

In Section 4 I will be sharing a useful self-help tool which will help you to change your limiting beliefs.

Now let's have a look at Exercise 6 to practise challenging a limiting belief.

EXERCISE 6 Challenging a limiting belief

Think of a key limiting belief that really affects you. You can choose one that you put a star against in Box 1 if you want.

Close your eyes and sit quietly for a few moments. Now say the limiting belief quietly to yourself a few times (for example, "I am useless"). Notice any emotion that comes up when you say it. You can also say any thoughts that comes into your mind when you are saying the limiting belief (ie "I hate myself for being useless", "Why do I have to be so useless", "There's something wrong with me", "No-one else is as useless as me" - notice how there are MORE limiting beliefs here!). Just keep repeating the belief and any thoughts about it until you feel calmer and the belief feels a bit less important.

Now find the opposite of the limiting belief (ie, "I am perfect") and say this a few times. Your mind will probably try and argue with what you are saying. Change it to a universal affirmation (ie, "I am perfection"). Notice that your mind is probably more accepting of this and saying it might even make your body feel softer and more relaxed. Keep repeating the universal affirmation until you feel more positive.

Follow the ongoing actions below so that you can continue to challenge your limiting beliefs.

Ongoing actions

- Repeat the above exercise for other key limiting beliefs.
- Every time you are having a bad day, see if you can spot which limiting beliefs are affecting you.
- Use positive affirmations and universal affirmations as much as possible for at least 30 days. This will help you programme in more positive beliefs to your subconscious mind.

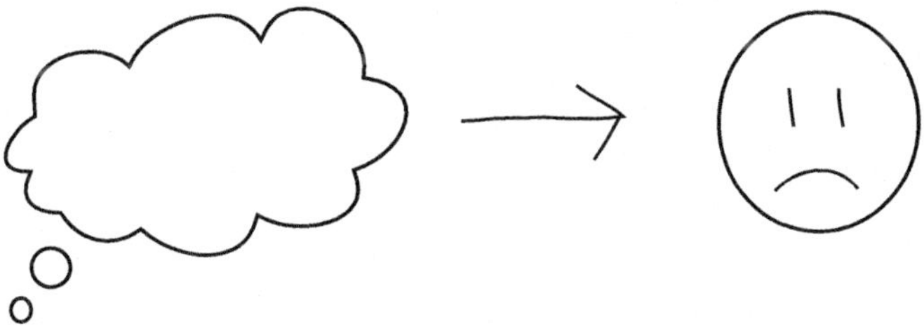

CHAPTER 3

How thoughts create feelings

So far in this section we have looked at the subconscious mind and also how we are affected by limiting beliefs.

Now we are going to look at how our thoughts create feelings. Before we do this, though, let's have a look at the stress response.

The stress response

In the past we would have had to guard against attack from wild animals and from also other tribes who were competing for land and food. When we were under attack we would feel frightened and our bodies would respond by releasing energising stress chemicals. This would help us to think better, run faster and fight better.

Life is pretty safe these days and the type of fear we tend to have now is more psychological or imaginary – are we behaving correctly in a social situation, are we performing well enough, how are others seeing us, are we going to be verbally attacked, is something bad going to happen to us in the future, etc.

But here's the thing:

➤ ***Your body can't tell the difference between real and imaginary danger.***

This means that if you are thinking negative thoughts about yourself or fearing or anticipating something in the future (ie an exam or a social situation you are not comfortable in), your body will respond to this imaginary danger in EXACTLY the same way it would respond to a real danger like being attacked.

Because your body THINKS you are in danger, it responds and releases stress chemicals to make it stronger and quicker. If there was a real live danger present, you would then burn up this excess energy by fighting or running away. But, as the danger is just imaginary, you just continue to sit and worry about it. Then, because the stress chemicals are not being burnt up, you would also start to get physical symptoms such as excess energy, a sick or tight feeling in your stomach, tense muscles and a racing heart. Sound familiar?

This would create a vicious circle as you would then start to worry about all the uncomfortable feelings you were now getting in your body. This would create EVEN MORE fear which would mean even more stress hormones would be released.

How thoughts create feelings

So we know that fear sets this stress response in motion in your body. But what causes the fear in the first place? Yes, you've guessed, it's coming from your thoughts. The body is so quick to adapt to your thoughts and create changes in your body that you probably wouldn't even notice that you had had a fearful thought, you would just say that you FEEL stressed. And the thoughts will probably be coming directly from your subconscious mind which means you wouldn't even be aware of them.

You would then make the decision that this stress has HAPPENED to you and would think "There is something wrong with me because I am feeling stressed". And, guess what, this creates even more negative thoughts and more feelings of stress.

BOX 3 Creating mental health issues

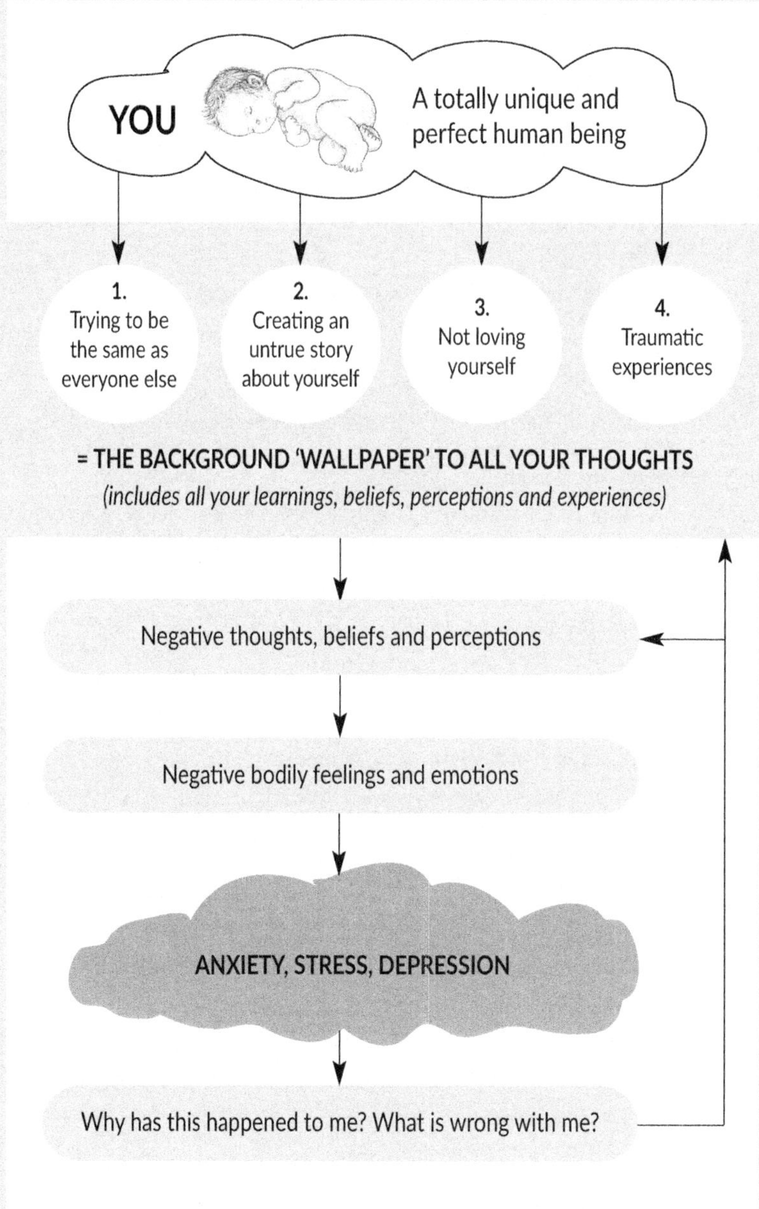

Let's summarise this as it is a bit complicated:

- Your wallpaper has a lot of limiting beliefs in it and you are really down on yourself.
- This gives you repetitive and anxious thoughts.
- Your body thinks you are in danger and so it prepares for fight or flight.
- This creates a feeling of tension and discomfort in your body.
- You then think "I FEEL stressed" and it becomes something that is 'happening' to you.
- You assume you are a powerless victim of this stress.
- This creates more negative thoughts such as "Why me?" or "There is something wrong with me".
- You become even more stressed and even more down on yourself.

Have a look at Box 3 on the previous page. It summarises the whole process in a more visual way. Box 4 opposite shows us how we can create happiness instead. Although these diagrams represent two extremes and most of us are somewhere in between, they are a useful reminder of how much our state of mind and our feelings are affected by our background wallpaper.

So, next time you feel really stressed, rather than beating yourself up about it, ask yourself what is going on in your thoughts. As stress is just a posh name for fear, ask yourself what you are frightened of. What is the worst thing that could happen? Is it actually happening right now or are you completely safe in this moment? Is it imaginary or real?

➤ ***Ultimately you will need to work on changing your wallpaper and your beliefs so that your subconscious does not constantly generate fear. Hopefully this book will help you to start to do that.***

Let's have a look at Exercise 7 to practise noticing the effect that different thoughts have on your body.

BOX 4 Creating happiness and peace

YOU

A totally unique and perfect human being

1. Being yourself and enjoying your gifts
2. Having a positive view of yourself
3. Loving yourself
4. Coping with whatever life brings you

= THE BACKGROUND 'WALLPAPER' TO ALL YOUR THOUGHTS

(includes all your learnings, beliefs, perceptions and experiences)

↓

Positive thoughts and perceptions

↓

Positive bodily feelings and emotions

↓

HAPPINESS, CONFIDENCE, PEACE

↓

I'm amazing and life is full of exciting possibilities

EXERCISE 7 How thoughts affect the body

Close your eyes and take a few deep breaths. How are you feeling right now? What are your thoughts like? Do you feel calm and relaxed? Does your body feel still and peaceful? Or perhaps you have lots of thoughts rushing around? How is this making your body feel? Is it tense? Are there any other symptoms?

Now I want you to think about something really stressful. Choose something from your life that really triggers you. If you can't think of anything, think of something frightening. Do this for a minute or so, really getting into the thoughts. Tune back into your body and see what is happening. What sensations are you getting?

Now focus on someone or something you really love, that makes you feel really happy. Breathe into this feeling and expand it into your body and allow it to fill your heart for a couple of minutes. Now see what is happening in your body? How does it feel? What sensations are you getting?

Does this exercise help you to see how different thoughts create different feelings in the body?

Complete the ongoing actions below to help you to become more aware of your negative and fearful thoughts.

Ongoing actions

- Next time you have any physical symptoms, see if you can work out what you are frightened of. Ask yourself if the fear is real or whether it's just psychological or imaginary.
- When you have negative feelings or symptoms, be aware that they are all being created by your thoughts. Stop seeing them as a wrongness, as something that is 'happening' to you.

CHAPTER 4

Listening to your body

In the last chapter we looked at how negative thoughts affect your body by activating the stress response. There's also a connection which goes from your body back to your mind. Let's have a look at this.

The body-mind feedback loop

Most people see the mind and the body as two separate things. But actually the brain is just another organ which means that the mind and the body are all part of the same body system. They communicate with each other through stuff like nerves and chemicals in the blood.

➝ ***They also communicate at a deeper more energetic level too. They know everything about each other and are totally connected.***

Therefore if your body is tense and stressed, your mind will know there is something wrong and this will make you feel more stressed. You can then get stuck in a circle of negative feedback going from mind to body and back to mind again.

A quick and easy place to temporarily stop feelings of stress and fear is by relaxing the body. So when things are really overwhelming and you recognise that you are having a lot of anxious thoughts, it can be helpful to do something physical such as breathing exercises, or yoga, or going for a walk or run.

I know adults often say that exercise makes you feel better and you have probably dismissed it as one of those boring things adults say, but it's actually TRUE. If you don't believe me, rate your stress level before you start some exercise and then again when you've finished. I bet it went down. Rate your happiness level too as I bet it will have gone up. It's also very good for your body to have exercise as it burns up the stress hormones, so it's a win-win situation.

Of course the good feelings will only be temporary as your mind will go back to generating fear once you have stopped exercising, but if you can do some exercise every day then it definitely makes a big difference and will give you regular breaks from your symptoms.

➤ ***It's good to know that there is something you can do to change the way you are feeling when you are in a really bad place.***

If you do tend to slip quickly back into fearful thoughts again after exercise, see if you can spot it happening. You might even be able to stop yourself doing it to some extent. Ask yourself whether the stress (ie fear) is real or imaginary and whether it's serving you in any way.

Finding meaning in your bodily sensations

You can also use your body to help spot more precisely what is going on in your wallpaper.

I follow a system called META-Health. The idea is that the body is adaptive and that it responds to our thoughts and feelings. It is always trying to make itself stronger and more effective to help you survive. Each part of the body has a specific function so if you are getting symptoms then it can give you clues about what you have been thinking and feeling.

Let's have a look at what some of the common physical symptoms might be showing you:

- **Racing heart and palpitations** shows that there is an excess of adrenaline. We also often get palpitations when we feel overwhelmed. What are you fearing? What are you making so big and why?

BOX 5 The power pose

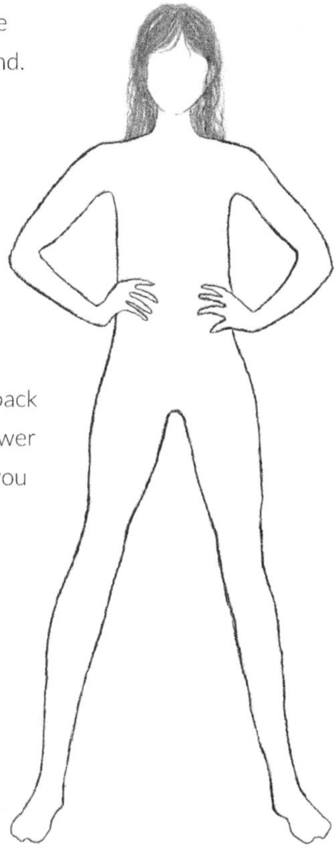

Your posture is a good example of the feedback loop between body and mind.

If you are feeling unhappy and unconfident then you might find that you hunch up and slightly curl into yourself. This is a protective thing but it also tells the brain that your body is weak and under threat.

If you stand tall with your shoulders back and head held high (known as the power pose), it makes your brain think that you are strong and powerful.

Have a go at it now. Stand upright and tall with your head up, your shoulders back, your legs apart and your hands on your hips. Be like a superhero! Then breathe in and out deeply, filling your lungs with air and expanding your body. Do this for a few minutes. How do you feel?

The power pose is useful if you have something stressful to do, like an exam, or a class presentation, or if you are meeting new people. Go to the toilet and do it for a few minutes and see how it changes things.

It can be hard to change your posture as it reflects how you feel inside, but if you keep practising the power pose it can have a big impact. The more we start feeding back to our minds that our bodies are relaxed and powerful, the more it becomes a reality.

- **Upper stomach problems** can show there is something you can't take in, digest, accept or process. What has happened that you just can't accept or make sense of? Stomach problems can also show that you are feeling a lot of anger, either actual or repressed. What is making you feel so angry and what it's really about? Is the anger hiding feelings of hurt or are you feeling frustrated about something?
- **Bowel problems** show there is something you can't let go of. What 'crappy' situation are you stuck in? What is stopping you letting it go?
- **Tight shoulders** can mean you feel burdened or that you are trying to protect yourself. What is going on for you? What burden are you carrying? What are you bracing against?
- **A clenched jaw** means you are holding a lot of tension. What are you worrying about? What can't you resolve or say?
- **Problems in the throat** can mean you are suppressing emotions or stopping yourself saying something. What are you not expressing? Why are you repressing your emotions?

If you want to find out more about META-Health, there's an article on my website at www.eleanorhatherley.com/other-resources.

Being more in touch with your body

It is really useful to learn to listen to your body more. Many of us just see it as a kind of disconnected physical thing that is there to do functional things for us like digesting food, moving us around. etc. But it is a big part of your whole being and you will be much happier if you live out of it more. If you look at little children, they are constantly and joyfully expressing their feelings with their bodies – running, skipping, jumping, dancing, stretching, singing, etc.

By getting out of our thinking brains and into our bodies we are able to connect with the animal part of ourselves. It helps us to deal with and process our emotions better and to listen to our instincts. This is a much healthier way of being than getting stuck in your head, with endless thoughts looping around and around.

➤ ***I am amazed by how many of my adult therapy clients don't know how to be in their bodies. They are SO stuck in their heads that they have totally lost touch with their bodies. They look at me blankly when I ask them where in their body they are feeling an emotion. Emotions have become a kind of horrible and dangerous energy that they have to stuff down.***

It's not helped by the fact that we spend a lot of time on computers and devices. Life is more and more about keeping our brains entertained and absorbed and less and less about being in our bodies.

This means we are living mainly out of our thoughts and our imaginations. It makes it much more likely that we will obsess over things that happened in the past, or create fearful future scenarios. We will also spend a lot of time thinking about things like how we look or how clever or popular we are. The more we use our brains, the stronger they get. Think of them like a muscle which we are constantly exercising.

If you can get more in touch with your body it will actually make you feel happier. I bet you didn't know this:

➤ ***Your body is always in the present moment.***

Yes, that's right, your body can't look ahead with imaginary thoughts and fear. It's anchored in the present moment, living through the senses (sight, sound, taste, touch and smell). THIS is where we should be living, not in our heads. Our brains are just tools for problem solving, not our homes.

So start to be more aware of where you are spending your time. Every time you remember, just check into your body. See what is going on there. Enjoy the sensations. This is you.

Let's look at Exercise 8 so you can practice connecting with your body.

EXERCISE 8 Connecting with your body

Sit quietly somewhere and take a few deep and slow breaths, in and out. Continue to do this and notice the sensation of your breathing in your body. Can you feel the air flowing in through your nose or mouth? Can you feel your ribs moving in and out? Can you feel your stomach and chest expanding? Are there any other sensations?

Now scan your body to see if there are any areas of tension or discomfort. Perhaps your stomach is churning or your throat feels tight? Perhaps your shoulders are stiff and aching? Find the area which is most uncomfortable and let your attention rest there.

Put both hands on that area and keep your attention there for a few minutes. Be aware of how much it's being affected by all your negative thoughts. You might even get a sense of what thoughts are creating the sensations. Perhaps something has happened that you can't let go of and your stomach is trying to digest it. Or perhaps you feel burdened by life and your shoulders are working hard to carry it.

You can repeat this on another area of the body if there are other areas of tension or discomfort.

Notice how you feel afterwards. Do you feel calmer? Do your thoughts feel stiller and less important?

Ongoing actions

- Repeat this exercise regularly to help you get in touch with your body more often. You can also do it when you are feeling very stuck in your head and your thoughts.
- Have regular exercise to help calm your mind.
- If you are getting any regular physical symptoms, try and work out what is going on in your thoughts.

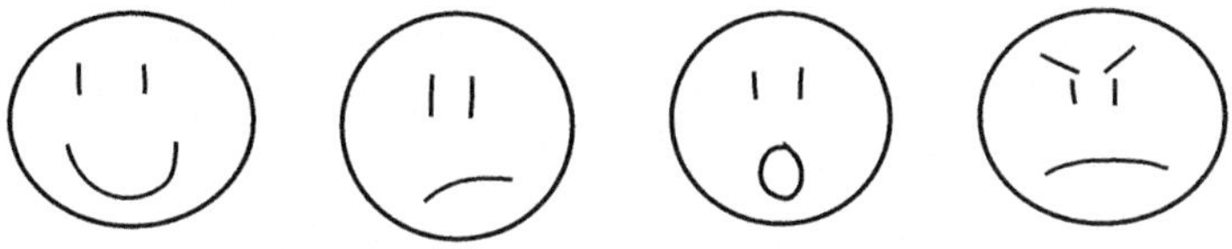

SECTION 3

Emotions

CHAPTER 1

All about emotions

A really important part of the mental health puzzle is emotions. Let's have a look at what they are, how they are supposed to work, why they often cause problems and what you can do about it.

What are emotions?

We all experience emotions and they are what make us human.

Emotions arise from the subconscious mind and then the body responds appropriately. For example, in the case of anger, the body goes into fight or flight mode to give us energy to express our anger and say what we need to say. We would then say that we 'feel' angry. In the case of happiness, the body would release feel good hormones which would relax our muscles and expand our breathing. We would then 'feel' happy.

But what controls which emotion arises from the subconscious mind?

We all have our own view of reality which is shaped by our wallpaper. Built into this are all our expectations and goals for ourselves and how we think the world around us should be. Our subconscious mind is constantly monitoring every situation to check that our expectations are being met.

If you come across something that doesn't fit with your expectations and beliefs then you will judge it as wrong, or frightening, or as something to resist or to put right in some way. The body then responds to this thought and gives you the appropriate chemicals and sensations to do this and you would feel an emotion like fear or anger.

If things go according to plan, or are even better than you expected, you would feel positive emotions like excitement or happiness.

➤ ***So it's not the things that happen that determine your emotions, it's your inner thoughts, perceptions, expectations and reactions.***

This means that we will all react a bit differently to the same situation. If, for example, you do badly in an exam, reactions can range from feeling sad ("I am so useless, nothing every goes right for me") to neutral ("Oh well, at least they are over now") to happy ("Yay! I did okay considering I did no work and if I just do a bit more next time I can do really well").

Repressing emotions 

Now we know how and why emotions arise, let's look at how they are supposed to work in the body.

We are designed for emotions to flow quickly through our whole body in quite a physical way so that we fully experience it inwardly and this moves us to act it out externally (ie shouting, crying, laughing). Once we have done both these things then that particular moment of emotion is finished.

The problem is that it's generally thought to be wrong to show your emotions too much, especially the more negative ones like anger.

If you look at a small children, they really express themselves fully with the whole range of emotions. An upset or angry child might hurl themselves on the floor, kicking and screaming. A really happy child might run around, arms out, making happy whooping noises.

Imagine if it was socially acceptable for us to fully express our emotions as they arise. Wouldn't it feel GOOD! Unfortunately we are taught to be socialised, not to get angry, not to shout, not to be too enthusiastic. We are taught to 'master' our emotions so we lose this natural ability to express ourselves.

It helps to keep society more civilised, but is it really good for us? Have we got it a little out of balance? Wouldn't it would be better if it was okay to express emotions but learn how to do it in a socially appropriate way?

Because it's considered wrong to express too much emotion outwardly we all end up a bit scared of our own emotions. We tend to judge ourselves for having so-called 'bad' emotions, as if there is something wrong with us. This means that we end up pushing them away instead and resisting them.

➛ ***Children often learn this way of dealing with their emotions from their parents. And, in the process of judging and repressing certain emotions, they are also learning to judge and repress parts of themselves.***

If we don't allow ourselves to feel and express our emotions then we end up repressing them. The emotions are then unfinished and they start to build up as they've got nowhere to go. And the only way to finish or complete the emotion is to FEEL it. We will look at how to do this later.

The problem is, when we have built up a lot of emotion because we haven't allowed ourselves to feel it, it feels like a massive bomb. It feels as if letting out even the tiniest bit of it will make you explode. And that feels scary so we avoid feeling it even more. But I promise you that in all the years I've worked as a therapist (and I deal mainly with helping people feel and release their emotions) that no one has ever exploded. The most I've seen is a bit of uncontrolled crying that lasts a few seconds.

➛ ***The body only ever releases a safe amount of emotion. It knows exactly how much you can deal with at any one time.***

Most people cry when they release emotions. The body is designed to work that way. The problem is that we think crying is wrong. We aren't comfortable crying in front of others. Some of us aren't even comfortable crying in front of ourselves! How about you? Are you okay to cry?

Some people release emotion by getting angry or by yawning or sighing. Others may need a physical activity, or to do something creative, or to play or listen to music. It's good to work out the best way to release emotions so you can then give your body plenty of opportunities to do this.

Emotional overwhelm

If we don't release our repressed emotions then every time something happens that triggers that emotion we can overreact. Imagine someone who has been suppressing anger for years. They will have a big pot of anger simmering away in their body. When someone annoys them it triggers the anger. The body thinks "Here's an opportunity to empty that pot of anger out a bit because it's getting so full". And it lets out as much as it dares, often out of proportion to what has triggered them. Do you recognise this pattern in anyone you know?

Let's summarise how we end up overwhelmed with repressed emotions as it's a bit complicated:

1. We are taught by society that certain emotions are wrong and so we don't want to experience them.
2. Emotions are designed to be felt and expressed and if we don't do this then they get stuck in our body.
3 The more we resist and repress them the more they build up in our bodies and the more uncomfortable we feel about them.
4. Eventually they get so big that we start feeling like we'll explode if we feel them so we avoid feeling them even more.
5. Every time that emotion gets triggered we overreact as the body is looking for opportunities to let some of it go.
6. This creates a pattern in that person and they will start to feel angry/sad/fearful more often.

If you are a teenager, this will be a particularly difficult time for you emotionally. Parts of your brain are developing and this means you will feel much more emotional than you used to, with your emotions swinging around wildly. But it will settle down and won't be like this forever.

Have a look at Exercise 9 to see how you handle your emotions.

EXERCISE 9 Exploring your emotions

Close your eyes and take a couple of deep breaths.

Ask yourself how you feel about your emotions. Are you comfortable with expressing them or do you tend to repress them? And how do you feel about other people's emotions?

If you are a very emotional person, is this because you naturally express your emotions when they come up, or is it because you often repress strong emotions which means you've got a big pot of emotion stored in your body so you are easily triggered?

If you are not very emotional, is this because you just aren't very emotional, or is it because you are repressing emotions? If you repress emotions, ask yourself why. Perhaps it doesn't feel safe, or socially acceptable, or you are ashamed of them, or you don't know how to express them? How does your family deal with them?

See if you can get a clear picture of your relationship with your emotions. Are you aware of any limiting beliefs that are affecting your emotions? Are these beliefs really true? Is there a better way to deal with your emotions in the future?

Follow the ongoing actions below so that you can start to improve your relationship with your emotions.

Ongoing actions

- Notice how you deal with your emotions on a day-to-day basis. Is it healthy? Could you do it better? Practice reacting differently.
- If you have a lot of repressed emotion then see if you can work out what is going on in your wallpaper to create it. Who are you angry at and why? Why are you sad? What is the story you are creating that is causing all this emotion?

*#$@&%!

CHAPTER 2

Expressing emotions

So far we have looked at what emotions are, how they are supposed to work and why they often cause problems. In this chapter we are going to look at how to express emotions better.

We all have emotions but, as we are all different, some people are much more emotional than others. There is no right or wrong so let's start by acknowledging how emotional you are (or aren't) and be okay with that.

Whether you are emotional or not, you do still have emotions and there are a few different ways that you might be dealing with them:

1. Expressing them very freely at all times with no judgement (this is very common for younger children but gets harder to do as you get older).
2. Expressing them freely in your family or with people you know well but repressing them at school or in other social situations.
3. Expressing safe and socially acceptable amounts of your emotions but repressing their full intensity.
4. Repressing your emotions most of the time because you have decided that they are not acceptable, or they make you feel out of control.
5. Finding it hard to get in touch with your emotions at all.

How emotional are you? What is your attitude towards emotions? How are emotions expressed in your family? How do you deal with your emotions?

Dealing with repressed emotions

As we learnt in the last chapter, many of us repress our emotions. This can be uncomfortable, especially if you are naturally a very emotional person. If you are less emotional then repressing your emotions can mean that you can lose the ability to feel your emotions at all. Neither of these are healthy and can contribute to poor mental health.

There is a big focus in our society on 'letting go of' or 'getting rid of' emotions, as if there is something wrong with them. But the only way to really let them go is to let them in to your body and FEEL THEM. They have to move right through you and be fully experienced without any resistance and then they will naturally subside. It's a very quick process.

Now the thought of letting strong emotions into your body might scare the life out of many of you. It's very common to be scared of feeling our own strong emotions. We are generally not happy with feelings of intensity or chaos and we also don't like feeling out of control. But I promise you don't need to be scared of your own emotions. Here are some useful facts:

- Emotions are just waves of energy and cannot physically harm you.
- There are no 'wrong' emotions, they are all natural and necessary.
- Your body will never let you feel more emotion than you can cope with.
- Resisting your emotions makes them feel stronger and more powerful.
- Feeling and releasing repressed emotions makes you feel much better.
- When you feel a repressed emotion it will just flash up for a few seconds.
- Being fully in touch with all your emotions makes you feel more alive.
- If you resist your emotions you are actually resisting parts of yourself.

The BAE technique

Now that you are (hopefully) more comfortable with the idea of feeling your emotions, we are going to learn something called the BAE technique.

Before we start, if you have a lot of repressed emotion or have experienced a big trauma, then this exercise could feel very intense.

It might make you cry uncontrollably for a few seconds. That's actually a good thing as you will feel much better afterwards. However, it can feel a bit scary the first time so you could ask someone to sit with you so you feel supported. Perhaps a parent or another relative.

Just remember, don't be scared of your own emotions – they can't hurt you. If they feel overwhelming then stop and walk around to discharge the energy. Then do some calming breathing. You can try the exercise again or, if it feels really uncomfortable, come back to it another time.

Others may have the opposite problem – getting in touch with any emotion at all. Don't worry if this is the case, just have a go anyway. The more you practice it the easier it will get. If you are really struggling with it then wait until you feel emotional about something and try again.

So, let's make a start. First you need to get in touch with a negative emotion that you want to work on (anger, fear, sadness etc). Once you can feel the emotion, follow these steps:

Be with the emotion, noticing where you can feel it in your body and what the sensations are.

Accept the emotion and any bodily sensations exactly as they are, without any judgement. Then say "It's okay to feel this".

Expand the emotion and the sensations so they grow and fill your body, flowing out of your fingertips, toes and the top of your head.

That's basically it. Nothing too difficult.

Once you know how to let your emotions move through you, you can make a habit of getting in touch with repressed emotions regularly. This will help you to feel more free from negative emotions.

Now let's do Exercise 10 to practice the BAE technique as we will be using it quite a bit in this book.

EXERCISE 10 The BAE technique

Think of a negative emotion that you struggle with – perhaps anger, fear, hurt or sadness. Then close your eyes and think of something or someone that makes you feel that emotion. Once you get in touch with the emotion, notice what sensations you are getting in your body. They will usually be somewhere like your stomach, throat, chest or shoulders. Or perhaps a general sensation in or around you.

Then just sit with the sensation of the emotion in your body. Don't analyse or judge it, just accept it. Relax your body and your thoughts, don't hold muscles tight against the feeling or try and stop it with your mind. Just watch the feeling in your body and let it do whatever it wants to do. Breathe it in and out. Let it unfold as if you are watching a film. Grow it bigger and stronger if you can.

Also be open to expressing it physically if that's what your body wants to do. You can move around, scream or make other noises (silently if you prefer). You might find yourself crying or shaking or curling into a foetal position. Whatever happens is perfect.

After a while you will start to feel lighter and it will get harder to feel the emotion. This might happen quickly or, if you are holding onto a lot of emotion, you might have to sit with these feelings for a while.

If at any point the exercise feels too intense then stop and walk around. Return to it when you feel calmer. You can get someone to sit with you or get professional help if you are really struggling.

Ongoing actions

- Practice this exercise every day to help clear emotions down. You can also use it when you feel really triggered by something.
- Once you have cleared out the pot a bit, experiment with how you deal with future emotions. Can you express them better?

CHAPTER 3

Clearing and managing emotions

So far we have looked at what emotions are, how they are supposed to work and how to express them. In this chapter we are going to look at how to clear emotions from traumas and how to deal with your emotions better in the future.

Emotions from traumas

Many of us find it difficult to really feel and express emotions because of past traumas.

Unprocessed traumas can lock strong emotions into our body and we can be scared to feel these emotions as they are a snapshot of how we felt when we were going through the trauma. We will try and avoid feeling them as much as possible as we don't want to re-experience the trauma.

➛ ***The best way to move out of a trauma and to let go of the emotions and other feelings that are stuck in your body is to FEEL them.***

Emotions have to be felt in your body, not your mind. You can rationalise as much as you want about why you had the trauma, why it made you feel like it did, how you'd handle it now, etc, but this emotional response comes from a more primitive part of the brain and it has to be discharged in a more primitive and animal way.

Let's have a go at visiting a trauma now. Choose one that isn't too big and feels safe for you to explore. DO NOT pick anything where you feel scared to even go there, or that brings up a lot of emotion, or that feels as if you have blocked out all your feelings when you think about it. You will need to get some help with these type of traumas. And if you do start working on a trauma and it feels overwhelming then STOP and get some support.

Once you have found a safe trauma to work with, follow these steps:

1. **Prepare.** Close your eyes and take a few deep, slow breaths. Get a sense of me being here to support you and know that you are completely safe right now. Be aware of your body and all its sensations.
2. **Connect with the trauma.** Think back to the trauma and see what happens in your body. If it's hard to get in touch with it then tell the story of the trauma, as if you were telling a friend. What do you feel in your body? What emotions come up? Just sit with whatever comes up and do the BAE technique. This will release some of the intensity.
3. **Express yourself physically.** When you think about the trauma, does your body wants to express itself? How would it like to move? Perhaps to cry, or to curl forwards, flail your arms around, punch, kick, run, scream, cry, etc. You can do all of this silently and in your imagination if that feels more comfortable. Try and stay out of your thoughts and don't judge what you are doing, just follow your body. It's very intelligent and will know what it needs to do to heal.
4. **Reframe the trauma.** Once you have released some of the emotional and physical energy from the trauma, see if you can see it in a different way. We experience early traumas in a very fixed way because we are young and don't have any perspective. Now you are older you can look at it differently. How would you react if it happened now? If you feel stuck, it can be helpful to talk it through with someone else as they will have a less emotionally charged view of it. Or see if you can think of someone who is very confident and happy in themselves - how would they handle the same trauma?

5. **Forgive.** Traumas sometimes involve someone else 'doing' something to us. We often hold on to feelings of anger or hurt and we won't be able to make peace with the trauma until we have forgiven the other person. This can be hard to do as it doesn't feel right to forgive them if they have done something really big to us. We want to hold onto our angry feelings as it makes us feel as if we are punishing them in some way. But actually we are only punishing OURSELVES. The other person doesn't care or even know that you are having these feelings. It is YOU that is suffering. Try and find a way of making peace with the situation. Do it for yourself, not for them.
6. **Identify any beliefs.** When we are young and we have a trauma, we form beliefs about ourselves and the world around us. For example, because of his public speaking trauma, Tom formed the belief that it was not safe to be seen. These beliefs become our future programming. See if you can spot what beliefs you might have formed from your trauma. Are they really true now that you have a more grown up perspective? Also see if you made any vows or promises ("I will never...", "I will always...")? Are these really serving you right now?
7. **Back in the present.** Come back into the room. Feel your body in the chair and take some deep and slow breaths.

It can take a bit of persistence to clear a trauma so it is worth repeating this process more than once. Additional details and feelings might come up another time. Use the process to clear as many traumas as you can.

Dealing with future emotions

It's good to learn a more healthy way of dealing with any future emotions that you might have.

The best way to do this is to feel and express them as they arise. So, for example, if someone makes you feel angry then express this to them. You don't have to shout and be over the top, just speak firmly and allow some of the anger energy to come through in your voice. And really allow yourself to feel the anger in your body. If you can't do this in public, take yourself off to the toilet for a few minutes and do it there.

It will feel difficult to express anger at first as you will probably be an expert in repressing it. You will probably also have lots of ideas about how people won't like you if you are angry. If it feels difficult, you could just start by noticing what you do when you feel anger in the moment. What happens in your mind and your body. How do you feel about the anger that is rising up in you? Are you okay with your anger or do you try and repress it?

➤ ***Start to practise reacting differently, taking baby steps.***

Anger is often a mask for hurt. It is easier to be angry with the other person than to really feel and own your hurt. When you feel anger arising, ask yourself whether you are really feeling hurt. If you are, make sure you fully feel and express these feelings. This will stop you getting so angry in the future.

Notice how you deal with other negative emotions too. How do they play out? What do you do with them? Then try something different. If you feel hurt, really allow yourself to feel the sensation of hurt. If you feel overwhelm or anxiety, allow the feeling of fear to fill your body.

Sometimes it's not appropriate to express an emotion when it comes up. For example, if a teacher tells you off and it makes you angry, or if a friend is really mean to you in front of lots of other people and you feel really sad. As soon as you can, find a quiet place and express it (by crying or punching the air or doing a silent scream). Get the feelings felt and out.

If you don't feel emotions very often then ask yourself why this is. You might naturally just be a person who doesn't have strong emotions (and that's fine). What are your parents like with their emotions? Is it a genetic pattern? Are emotions generally repressed in your family? Perhaps you learnt from a young age that you wouldn't be loved if you expressed negative emotions? Or perhaps you always like to be in control of yourself? Try and see whether deep down you'd like to be more emotional. What does your happy younger self think?

➛ ***As well as negative emotions, we are often not very good at expressing happy emotions. How do you act when you are really happy? Can you express your happiness more?***

Remember that strong emotions arise from your subconscious so you will also need to keep working on this.

Now let's do Exercise 11 to learn a visualising technique which will help you to release and express pent up emotions.

EXERCISE 11 Releasing emotions

We are going to do some visualising in this exercise. If you find it very hard to visualise clearly then don't worry, just do your best.

Close your eyes and think of someone who makes you feel angry or who has hurt you. Really get in touch with the feelings.

Then imagine a little scene with you and that other person. Put them on freeze and really act out the emotions you are feeling. Go crazy! You can punch and kick, shout, scream, cry, curl into a ball, whatever feels right. Say all the things you need to say. Really express yourself.

When you feel a bit calmer, imagine you are holding a big glowing white ball of peace. Split this into two and place half of it in your chest and half in their chest. Unfreeze them and stand facing each other. Just focus on the two glowing white balls. If you still feel too angry or hurt to do this then put them on freeze and go back to acting out your emotions again. Then try again.

Once you feel comfortable with the energy of the glowing white balls, expand them until they merge together and fill the whole scene with white glowing peace. Sit with this energy for a few minutes, really feeling it. Then slowly come back into your own body and open your eyes.

Follow the actions below to help you to release unwanted emotions and to deal with them differently in future:

Ongoing actions

- Repeat the above exercise every time you feel strong negative emotions towards anyone else.
- Practice really feeling your emotions rather than resisting them.
- Keep working on clearing emotions from traumas.

CHAPTER 4

Negative emotions

Now we understand emotions a bit better, I thought it might be useful to have a look at 'negative' emotions in more detail.

As human beings, we experience a whole range of different emotions, from total joy and bliss to complete desolation or terror. They are a very important part of being human and without them we would be robotic.

As we have already seen, in our society we believe that some emotions are good and others are bad. But ALL emotions are equally valid and important and, as human beings, we have been designed to feel them all.

Let's have a look at each of the more negative emotions so we understand them better. If you are constantly experiencing one particular emotion, this will help you to see what might REALLY be going on for you.

Anger 

Anger is a powerful emotion which floods our body with energy and makes us shout or even lash out physically. It would have been a useful survival tool when we were cavemen but it's harder to manage in modern society.

It's useful for defining our boundaries and for protecting our integrity. If used in the right way then it makes us powerful and respected.

But when we are angry we often lose control of ourselves and can end up saying hurtful things. If you are a sensitive person then you can regret showing this 'bad' side of yourself and you might feel upset that you hurt someone. Next time you feel angry you will therefore tend to repress it.

When we repress anger it often comes out later when we are with people we feel safe with (parents or siblings). It can be triggered over something really small and is often out of all proportion. It can also come out as bitterness, sarcasm, coldness or hostility. All of this can really affect your relationships with your family and friends, making everyone miserable.

➤ ***Anger can also be repressed so much that you never allow yourself to feel or act on it again. This can lead to other mental health issues such as depression and anxiety.***

If you feel angry a lot, there will definitely be something behind it. Here are a few reasons why you might be getting angry regularly:

- Anger is often a mask for other emotions, such as hurt. Hurt might come from feeling unloved, ignored, unimportant, unfairly accused or rejected. The anger covers up feelings that are too painful or too difficult to feel or express. It is easier to make the other person wrong instead. Next time you feel angry, ask yourself what the emotion is behind the anger. Where does it come from? Why are you feeling it?
- Anger can also be about frustration or irritation. Perhaps you are not getting what you want, not being listened to or not feeling respected by your parents or someone else close to you? See if you can find a calmer way to communicate with them about how you are feeling, rather than just getting angry. Perhaps you can both make some compromises. Parents can find it hard to change their behaviour so keep persevering.
- As anger gives us a boost of energy, some people use it to feel and appear powerful. If this is you, remember that anger is not good for your body. There are better ways to feel powerful. Ask yourself why you don't feel powerful in the first place. The more you get back in touch with who you really are and drop all the negative stories and beliefs, the more you will find that you don't have to be angry to feel powerful.

So how should we deal with anger? Ideally we should just express it in an honest way each time it comes up. I know people who do this and it works surprisingly well. Because the anger always gets expressed, it doesn't build up so it always comes out in a manageable way. The people around them are used to them being like this and they know where they are with them. They tend to be respected and they have good boundaries.

To operate like this will probably be a bit of a process for most of us. You will need to start by becoming aware of what your anger is really about. Is it masking an underlying emotion like hurt, frustration or powerlessness? What or who triggers you and why? Once you understand your patterns, notice your anger and practice dealing with it differently.

➛ ***If you experience a lot of anger, find a physical way to vent it. Go to a boxing club, do some vigorous exercise, or express it through music or creativity. This will help you to get the anger out of your body.***

Fear

Fear causes physical changes in the body to prepare us for fight or flight. It is a useful emotion as it protects us from danger.

The problem is, as I have already mentioned, the body cannot tell the difference between real and imaginary fear. Most of our fear is imaginary or psychological these days as our environment is pretty safe.

We have to protect our self, our reputation and our image. We have to guard against verbal attacks and the opinion of others. We also feel as if we have to constantly perform well so we don't fail or get rejected.

We also create fear by anticipating how things are going to be in the future. We create detailed and imaginative stories about what is going to happen and how it's going to feel. We make it feel so real that our bodies think it's actually happening in that moment.

So what's the best way to deal with fear?

Start by asking yourself "Am I safe right now?". Then ask "What is the very worst thing that could happen?". It might be a fear of something specific or of feeling something you don't want to feel. When you have an answer, ask "And what is the worst thing about that?" Keep digging down until you find the core of the fear. We will practice this in Exercise 12.

Then see if you can work out the underlying cause. Fear can be a result of stuff like low self esteem or limiting beliefs so really look at your wallpaper.

➤ ***There can also be a trauma at the root of it. Ask yourself when the fear started and what was happening in your life at the time.***

It's also good to practice really feeling and acknowledging your fear, especially if it's to do with not wanting to experience certain emotions or feelings. Use the BAE technique. Just sit with it and allow your fear to fill your whole body. Don't judge or resist it. This will all help to make it smaller.

Embarrassment

Embarrassment causes a hot, overwhelmed, uncomfortable feeling. We feel exposed, awkward and powerless, as if we've done something wrong or stupid. It happens when we feel as if we have not behaved in an appropriate way, or when we are on the end of undesired attention.

➤ ***It's interesting that we only experience embarrassment in social situations and rarely, if ever, feel embarrassed when we are on our own. It shows that worrying about what others think is at the root of it.***

Ask yourself what is behind your embarrassment. For example, if you feel embarrassed when you have to speak in class you are probably worried about how you will come across or of getting the answer wrong. Dig into your wallpaper and see why you are feeling like this and what's behind it.

Embarrassment can also be triggered by traumas. For example, if you feel uncomfortable and embarrassed when you stand up and speak in front of the class, perhaps something went wrong when you were in a similar situation in the past and some repressed emotions are trying to come up?

Ultimately embarrassment is overcome by fully being yourself and not caring what others think.

Sadness

We often feel sadness when we lose someone we love, or we are rejected, or someone is unkind to us, or someone we love is suffering.

➛ ***Sadness is bitter sweet and it's also compassionate. The ability to feel sadness makes us deeper and richer as human beings. We have to experience sadness to really experience happiness.***

If you are feeling a lot of sadness, there may be an obvious reason. Perhaps you have lost someone close to you. It's good and natural to feel sadness and to express it. Cry as much as you can and let it out. The more you feel it, the quicker it will pass.

Sometimes we are sad but it gets stuck inside us because we are pushing it down and resisting it. Really try and get in touch with the sadness by using the BAE technique. If you find it hard to feel it, it might be helpful to talk to someone close to you as talking is a good way to let stuff out. Or you could work with a therapist if you feel really stuck.

If you often feel sad but don't really know why, it's possible something has happened to you in the past that made you feel sad but you pushed it down. Then every time the tiniest opportunity comes up to feel sad, your body will try and express some of it. Ask yourself what might have happened. What was going on in your life when your sadness started? Really try and get in touch with your repressed feelings.

Hurt

Hurt is a vulnerable feeling where we feel worthless or unloveable. This is a deep and painful feeling and we tend to not want to feel it. To avoid feeling it we quickly cover it up with anger and blame ("I never liked her anyway, she's a bitch").

We also don't want other people to see our feelings of hurt as it doesn't feel safe to show our deepest vulnerability. Ironically it actually makes us more likeable if we show vulnerability. We seem more human. Who do you like most, people who always seem perfect and in control, or people who are more open and admit when they feel hurt and vulnerable?

Hurt shows us that deep down we have a problem with our self worth. If you really believed in yourself you wouldn't be bothered about what other people said or did to you.

➤ ***If you really loved yourself it wouldn't matter if others didn't.***

So if you feel hurt a lot then ask yourself how you feel about yourself deep down. Why are others able to hurt you so easily? Next time you feel hurt, really feel and own the hurt.

Shame 

Shame is a kind of creeping uncomfortable feeling. It's also quite a vulnerable feeling. It happens when we have decided that parts of ourself are not acceptable or loveable. If this part of ourself is revealed then we feel very ashamed. What will people think of us? Will they like us now they've seen this terrible part of us?

The reality is that no one else cares. They are too focused on their own stuff and, actually, as I've already said, people tend to like you more when you are vulnerable. It connects us in a heartfelt way. It often makes other people feel better about their own stuff too when others are openly vulnerable.

So if you often feel shame then it's showing you that you are judging yourself and have made a decision that something about you is wrong. Remember, nothing about you is wrong because we are all different. What is happening in your wallpaper to make you feel as if something is wrong with you? What untrue story have you created about yourself?

Sometimes we DO do something wrong. We then regret it and feel very ashamed. But it's done and you can't change it. If you are feeling shame then you know it was wrong so stop beating yourself up. You need to forgive yourself, learn from the mistake and move on.

Envy

Envy is where we find ourselves wanting what others have rather than focusing on all the good things we have. It usually comes from a lack of self worth and wanting to be like others. It shows you that you don't value yourself and that you are comparing yourself with others.

Perhaps you want certain traits (to be more attractive, more intelligent, more popular etc)? Ask yourself honestly whether you have made up an untrue story about yourself (perhaps you already have these traits?), or whether you are wanting traits that you will never have because you are not honouring who you are but are trying to be like others.

Perhaps you want more of something materialistic (money, clothes, gadgets, etc)? Ask yourself why it is so important to you to have these things. What will having them make you feel? Why can't you feel like this anyway? Dig deep and see what the real reason is that you want these things. Where are you REALLY lacking? Perhaps you feel unloved so you buy things to treat yourself and feel more special? Perhaps you feel lonely so you want all the latest games and equipment to keep you company? Perhaps you feel unattractive so you buy clothes to feel prettier?

Guilt

Guilt is a negative feeling of regret. We feel as if we should have done or be doing something differently.

It's usually based on people pleasing, on being too concerned by what others think of us. We feel a need to keep everyone around us happy and to meet their expectations and we feel guilty if we don't.

For example, if we forget someone's birthday, we might feel guilty that we forgot. We might think things like "I wish I'd tried harder, I'm useless". However, it wasn't intentional so really there is nothing to feel bad about. A quick heartfelt apology is all that is needed.

➤ ***Don't beat yourself up. Learn from your mistake if you can or need to, then stop being hard on yourself.***

Guilt can also be caused by a conflict between doing what you really want to do and doing what you know someone else wants you to do. If you do what the other person wants you to do, you won't feel guilty but you can end up feeling angry or resentful instead as you didn't get what you wanted.

So if you feel guilty a lot, why are you beating yourself up so easily? Why are you so concerned about what others think of you? Why is it more important to please others that to be true to yourself?

Next time you feel guilty, stop and check why. Are you being hard on yourself? Are you people pleasing? Are you worried that people won't like you if you don't please them? Dig deep and see what is behind all of this.

Hate

Hate is a strong emotion that is a bit like anger. There is usually a lot of emotion and passion behind hate. It's useful for expressing our displeasure and for showing other people what is not acceptable.

It usually covers up other things like hurt and poor self worth. For example, if we fall out with a friend we'll often say "I really hate her". We don't really hate them but we have lots of strong and complicated emotions and hate is an easy way of transferring all the blame onto them.

So next time you feel as if you hate someone, ask yourself what the REAL emotions are. Are you actually feeling hurt or perhaps rejected deep down? It's much easier to direct hatred at them than to look inside.

➤ ***It's always better to try and forgive people or find a way to move forwards. Hatred is a very negative and destructive emotion and is not good for you.***

We also sometimes hate things (school, our bodies, ourselves, rules etc). It's a complete waste of time to do this. It's just setting up a pattern of resistance which is bad for your health and doesn't make you happy. Ask yourself why you hate these things. Is the hate really a mask for something else - hurt, feeling inadequate, powerless etc?

Loneliness

Loneliness is a sad empty feeling where we feel as if we are not loved or connected to other people.

It might be showing us that we need to get out and spend more time with other people. Human being are naturally sociable (although some more than others). If you have plenty of company but you still feel lonely then it could be showing you that you are spending time with the wrong people.

Another reason people feel lonely is that they lack the confidence to seek out friendships. It's usually a protective thing. Perhaps you have been hurt or rejected in the past and you don't want to risk feeling this way again so it feels safer to just shut down and avoid people. But, although it can protect you, it is a miserable way to live. Ask yourself why you have shut down and what you are protecting yourself from feeling. Why are you letting something someone once did to you or said to you affect you so much? Have a look at your wallpaper to see what is really going on. And really feel any emotions from any past hurts.

➤ ***Once you value yourself more then you will find it easier to connect and you will feel less lonely.***

Other emotions

If you are experiencing a strong emotion which isn't in this chapter then think about what might be behind it. It's usually stuff like fear or poor self worth. Try and see what is really going on in your wallpaper.

Any 'negative' emotion that you experience a lot will be very useful for giving you pointers about where your thinking is skewed and where your wallpaper needs attention.

Complete Exercise 12 to practice a technique for getting to the bottom of negative emotions.

EXERCISE 12 "What's behind this?"

Choose the negative emotion that you feel the most. Then close your eyes and really get in touch with this emotion. See if you can feel it in your body. Totally accept the feeling and let it grow, filling your whole body, as we did in the BAE technique.

Once it feels calmer, ask yourself "What's behind this emotion?". Something may immediately pop into your mind – an image, another emotion, a bodily feeling, a thought, or even a memory. Whatever comes up, just repeat the process again, totally accepting the thing or feeling and allowing it to fill your body and then asking again "What's behind this?". Keep repeating this until you reach a feeling of peace. Sit for a while and really feel this sense of peace.

This process can go on for quite a while and all sorts of strange stuff can come up. Let your imagination do whatever it needs to do and don't let your thoughts get in the way. It's a very useful way of working with your subconscious mind.

Don't worry if you find this process hard to do. It can take practice and, if you aren't very visual, you might struggle with it. If you find it hard, ask someone else to help. All they need to do is keep asking "And what's behind that?" and prompting you to really feel whatever comes up. It's quite fun to do together and you can swap afterwards.

Follow the ongoing actions to help you with your negative emotions.

Ongoing actions

- Use the above exercise to help you get behind any strong emotions that you regularly feel.
- Notice when you get negative emotions and see if you can work out what is really going on.

SECTION 4

A useful self-help tool

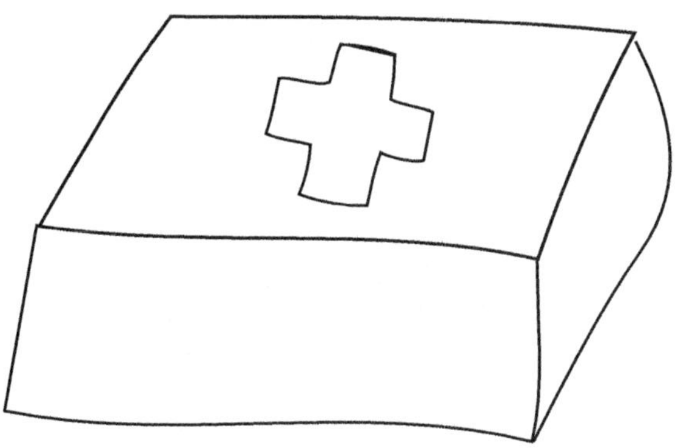

CHAPTER 1

Mastering the basics

Are you starting to see how not being yourself, making up untrue stories, not loving yourself and having unprocessed traumas, combined with limiting beliefs, negative thoughts and repressed or badly managed emotions can lead to poor mental health?

Hopefully you are starting to feel clearer about what might be going on for you?

A useful self-help tool 

Even if you are starting to see things differently, changing your deepest subconscious thoughts, perceptions, beliefs, emotional reactions and traumas can be difficult. Many people continue to get really caught up in the energy of it all even when they consciously understand what is going on. To help you with this, I am going to share a really useful tool.

Known as EFT (Emotional Freedom Techniques), or 'tapping', it can help you:

- Clear strong emotions and feelings
- Change how you feel in the moment about yourself or a situation
- Get rid of limiting beliefs
- Uncover and clear traumas
- Reduce or clear physical symptoms

EFT has been around for nearly 40 years and it's getting more and more popular. Many therapists use it and it's also used in the performance and sports industries. There is quite a bit of research around which shows that it's very effective (see www.evidence.nhs.uk/search?q=emotional%20 freedom%20technique).

EFT is very simple and effective and the best thing about it is that you can use it on yourself. It's one of the main therapy tools that I use and I really love it. It can be used at different levels – an experienced EFT therapist will use it to make deep and core changes, but it's also very effective when you use it at a simpler and more surface level on yourself.

Once you have learnt it, you will always have a useful tool which you can use in the moment. This can be a real life saver when things feel really difficult. I honestly don't know how I would live without it.

Let's have a look at how it works. It may seem complicated (and definitely a bit weird!) but it's really simple once you've done it a few times.

How to tap

There are four steps to using EFT:

- STEP 1: Deciding what to work on
- STEP 2: Creating a set-up sentence
- STEP 3: Tapping
- STEP 4: Checking back in

Let's look at each of these steps in turn.

STEP 1: Deciding what to work on

You can tap on ANYTHING with EFT but it's usually used on something that is very present for you in that moment that is bringing up strong emotions or feelings. You can also use it to work on something from the past, or a limiting belief or pattern.

For now we are going to pick something general so that you can learn the technique. We will use the expression "I feel stressed". Hopefully you can all relate to this. If you can't, try making it a bit more specific – "I feel stressed about... (ie my exams, the argument I had with my friend, how I look, etc)". Find something that feels really true for you.

Close your eyes and take a couple of long slow breaths. Rate how true the statement feels out of 10 (0 being not true at all and 10 being really true).

STEP 2: Creating a set-up sentence

We now need to create a set-up sentence about the problem. We always start every set-up sentence with "Even though..." and end it with "I'm okay". So this one would be "Even though I feel stressed, I'm okay".

Using the middle three fingers of your writing hand, tap gently on the little finger side of the other hand. This is known as the Karate Chop point (see Box 6). Tap lightly at a speed to suit you (roughly two to four taps per second) while saying the set-up sentence out loud, "Even though I feel stressed, I'm okay".

Repeat this three times out loud. Try and really connect with the words. You might find it makes you feel a bit emotional – that is great as it shows it's working. Or it might just feel silly. That's fine too.

BOX 6 The Karate Chop point

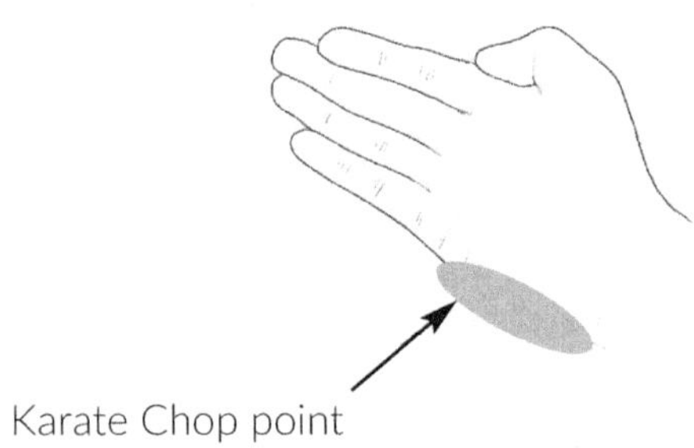

BOX 7 The tapping points

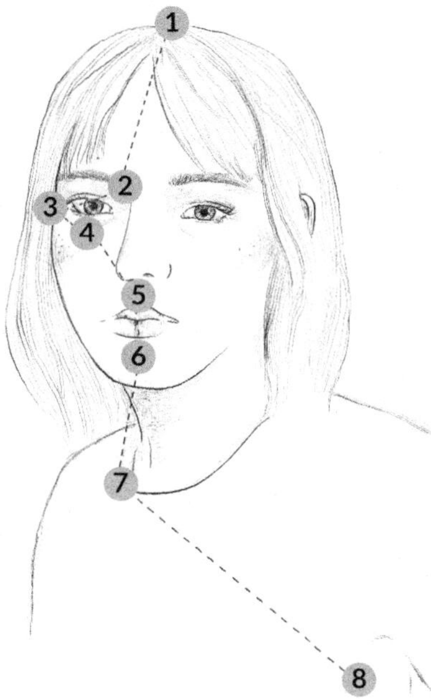

1. Top of the head
2. Inner eyebrow
3. Side of the eye
4. Under the eye
5. Under the nose
6. Chin dip
7. Collarbone
8. Under the arm

STEP 3: Tapping

We are now going to tap on some points on the face and body. These are acupuncture points and tapping on them calms your brain and helps to release any trapped emotions.

We will be tapping on each point roughly seven times, saying "I feel stressed" when you get to each point (you don't need to say "Even though", or "I'm okay" when you tap on the points). You can tap on either side of the body. It doesn't have to be exact and you can't get it wrong.

Here are the tapping points (see Box 7). Tap on each point and say "I feel stressed":

1. Top of the head
2. Start of the eyebrow on the nose side
3. Side of the eye (on the bone)
4. Underneath the eye (on the bone)
5. Between the nose and the mouth
6. The middle of the chin (in the dip which is halfway between the mouth and bottom of your chin))
7. Collarbone (find the dip at the bottom of your throat and move down about two inches and then out towards your shoulder by two inches)
8. Under the armpit (level to the nipple)
9. Top of the head again

It feels complicated but once you know where the points are you can do it automatically without thinking. Practice tapping around a few times (without any words). Even doing just this might make you feel calmer.

STEP 4: Checking back in

Take a deep breath and tune back into the original problem ("I feel stressed"). See how you are feeling now about it. It might still feel the same or it might have changed a bit. There is no right or wrong answer so just see how it feels. Rate the feeling out of 10 again, just going with the number that pops into your head.

Practising the basic round

At this point you would usually do another round, adjusting the set-up phrase to match how you are now feeling. However, for now, I want you to just practice the same round a few more times until you feel really comfortable with the process.

So, staying with your original phrase, "I feel stressed" (or whatever you used), practice the whole thing again from Step 2 through to Step 4. Here's a quick summary:

BOX 8 Summary of the basic EFT round

STEP 1
Decide what the problem is that you want to work on and rate it out of ten

I feel stressed

9/10

STEP 2
Tap on the side of your hand while saying the set-up sentence three times

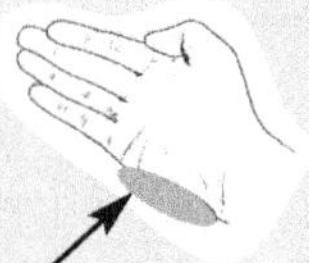

+

"Even though I feel stressed, I'm okay"

STEP 3
Tap roughly seven times on each point while saying the reminder phrase

+

"I feel stressed"

STEP 4
Tune back in to see how you feel now about the problem and rate it out of ten

"I still feel stressed, but not as much"

6/10

- STEP 2: Say the set-up phrase “Even though I feel stressed, I’m okay” three times out loud while tapping on the side of your hand.
- STEP 3: Tap through all the points (roughly seven taps on each point) saying the reminder phrase “I feel stressed” at each point.
- STEP 4: Tune back in and rate how you feel about the problem out of 10.

Repeat Steps 2 to 4 until you have really mastered the basic round and are comfortable with where all the tapping points are. You might find that your number drops but don’t worry if it doesn’t as we are just practising.

Evolving the problem

Once you feel more confident with the tapping, let’s keep working on the original problem (“I feel stressed”) and see if we can evolve it more.

Close your eyes and tune back in to see how you feel now. You might still feel stressed but the feeling might not be as strong (“I still feel stressed but it feels a bit better”), or the problem may have opened up into something more specific (“I feel stressed because I’m going to fail my exams”, or “I feel stressed because I haven’t got any friends”). Or something completely different might have come up (“I feel really angry”). It might even be “This tapping is stupid and won’t work for me”!

All you need to do is to see how you are feeling right now, there is no right or wrong answer. Imagine someone asking you “How do you feel?”. Then create a new set-up sentence based on that (eg, “Even though I feel..., I’m okay”). We are going to do another round, following Steps 2 to 4 again:

- STEP 2: Say the set-up phrase you have chosen three times out loud while tapping on the side of your hand (Karate Chop point).
- STEP 3: Tap through all the points (roughly seven taps on each point) saying the reminder phrase at each point.
- STEP 4: Tune back in and rate how the problem feels now out of 10.

When you have finished this round, ask yourself again how you are feeling. Then create a new set-up sentence based on this and tap on it, following

Steps 2 to 4. Keep repeating this process, following your feelings, until you feel more peaceful and the original problem doesn't feel like such a big deal. You can do as many rounds as you want.

➣ ***If you are finding the tapping difficult or confusing, you can watch a short tapping video at www.youtube.com/watch?v=pAclBdj20ZU by Jessica Ortner who is a well known EFT practitioner. It's a nice clear demo of how to tap. You will notice that she does the tapping in a slightly different order to me as she starts with the eyebrow point rather than the top of the head, and she also says "I love and accept myself" rather than "I'm okay". As we will see in the next chapter, you can vary the process.***

Keep practising the tapping until it feels really comfortable. We are going to look at some more tips and techniques in the next chapter to improve your tapping but make sure you are confident with the basics first.

CHAPTER 2

Improving your skills

Once you have mastered the basics, there are lots of ways to get more from your tapping. Let's look at some of these now.

Getting the set-up sentence just right

The more specific and accurate the set-up sentence is, the better the EFT will work.

For example, if you are feeling angry because of an argument with a friend, rather than just saying "I feel angry" you could say "Even though I feel really angry because my friend was mean to me, I'm okay". Or try and see what the real emotions are under the anger "Even though my friend has made me feel like I'm unlovable, I'm okay". Or even "Even though this keeps happening to me and I'm scared I'll never be happy, I'm okay".

You will know if you get the set-up phrase right as you will feel some emotion come up inside you when you say it. Test a few out loud before you start and see if you can get the exact right words.

If you are finding it hard to come up with something then ask yourself "What's the very worst thing about this situation?". This question helps you get to the bottom of the problem and to work out what is bothering you the most about it. For example, if you've had an argument with a friend, the worst thing might be that you are scared you'll lose the friendship.

Acceptance

One of the most important things about EFT is that it helps us to accept and acknowledge things we are feeling. Remember, as we have already seen when we looked at how emotion works, the minute we really accept something rather than fighting it off then the energy of the thing we are fighting off will get lower and we won't feel so bothered about it.

This acceptance is built into the set-up sentence ("I'm okay") but you can make it stronger by saying "I accept myself" or "I accept myself and all my feelings" or even "I deeply and completely love and accept myself and all my feelings".

Being flexible

There is no right or wrong with the tapping. You can tap on either side of the body, alternate between the two sides, miss points out, do them in a different order, stay on one point for longer, just tap on one point, etc. You can also leave the actual tapping out. And you can tap by imagining you are tapping and saying the words in your head (useful in a public place).

You can also change the words halfway through a round if they don't feel right or the problem evolves. Something might pop into your mind halfway through a round that feels important so change to that. Be creative and flexible. Don't be scared of it.

You can also throw in different things when you are doing a tapping round. See it like a good old rant as you tap around the points. So, using the example above where you had an argument with a friend, rather than just saying "I feel angry" all the way through the round, say stuff like:

Top of the head – "I feel angry"
Inner eyebrow – "My friend was so mean"
Side of the eye – "Why are people always so mean to me"
Under the eye – "I've had enough of it"
Under the nose – "All this anger"
Chin dip – "It makes me feel sick"

Collarbone – "I hate feeling so angry"
Under the arm – "I hate mean people"

Body work

Rather than tapping on your feelings and emotions, you can tap on sensations in your body. This gets us in touch with the subconscious mind.

Tapping on body sensations is useful when you:

- Have a physical pain or any other physical symptoms
- Are struggling to work out what you are feeling upset about
- Find it difficult to get in touch with or express your emotions

Let's try it now. Close your eyes and scan your body. Look for any tight or uncomfortable areas or any stress sensations. Then describe the sensation (ie a swirling feeling in my stomach, a tight feeling in my throat). Ask yourself if the sensation were to have a colour what it would be.

We are now going to create a set-up sentence. For example "Even though I have this swirling red feeling in my stomach, I'm okay". Or "Even though I have this tight black blocked feeling in my throat, I'm okay".

➤ ***It's useful to give feelings a colour. It helps to express how your subconscious is feeling. Black often shows that there is fear, red indicates anger, blue might be sadness and grey perhaps something like emptiness.***

Do a tapping round using your set-up sentence and then see how that place in your body feels. It should have changed but the changes could be quite subtle (a bit paler, a bit smaller). If it hasn't changed then do another round. Once it does change, adjust the set-up statement and tap again. For example "Even though I have a cloudy pale red feeling in my stomach, I'm okay" or "Even though I have a light grey tight feeling in my throat, I'm okay".

The sensation might even move somewhere else in your body "Even though I have a black heavy feeling in my chest now, I'm okay". Just follow the sensations in your body and keep repeating the process until you start to feel better and your body feels lighter and more relaxed.

➤ ***This process is a really good way of releasing pent up emotions. You don't have to go into the story, just follow the sensations in your body.***

Positive statements

EFT is unusual because we work on negative statements. It can seem as if we are making our problems bigger by saying them out loud. This is actually not true. The problem with most feelings is that we are resisting them. By saying the feeling out loud and by adding "I'm okay" onto the end it reminds us that we are bigger than our problems. It allows us to accept and acknowledge the problem which will immediately reduce it.

However, if the tapping doesn't seem to be shifting the negative feelings then it can be helpful to add some positive phrases into your tapping. Start by doing a round or two on the negative thing and, when you are starting to feel a bit better, replace the usual sentence with something like:

- "Even though I feel useless, I am open to the possibility that I'm amazing."
- "Even though I'm weird, maybe I could learn to enjoy my weirdness."
- "Even though I feel sad all the time, I know that I am working hard on it and it will change in time."
- "Even though I feel really stuck, I deserve to feel better."

You can make up anything that feels right – get creative! But make sure you clear the negative feelings down a bit though before you introduce the positive suggestions or your mind will try and argue with it.

Positive EFT

Positive EFT is good to do at the end of a tapping session after you have cleared out negative stuff. It will leave you feeling really good.

Start by thinking of a quality you want to have. This can be anything but common ones might be courage, happiness, energy or peace. You can also choose the quality of another being or thing – for example, waterfall energy or superhero energy. Once you have chosen your quality, find another word or a colour to describe it. For example, "yellow happiness", "pale blue peace", "lion courage", "energising waterfall energy".

Now close your eyes and put your hands on the centre of your chest. Using yellow happiness as an example, say "I would like yellow happiness". Then take slow three breaths. Now tap around the points, saying your statement each time. You can vary it a bit, saying things like "I want even more yellow happiness", "Filling my whole body with yellow happiness", "Filling every cell of my being with yellow happiness". Do the tapping slowly and take a slow deep breath after each statement. Really connect with the quality.

What to do when the tapping isn't working

EFT tends to work even if you don't believe in it. However, very occasionally it doesn't work. This can happen if:

- You are taking antidepressants or other medication.
- You find it really hard to tune in to your emotions.
- You have shut yourself right down because of a trauma.
- You are blocking the process with your mind because deep down you don't really want to change.

  ➤ ***I once had a client who had depression. We found that deep down she didn't want to let go of the depression because that would mean she'd have to go back to work and be responsible for her life again. It kind of felt good to have people looking after her and being a bit helpless and not having to do much.***

Try doing a few rounds on the problem of the EFT not working, selecting one of these options as your set-up sentence (see which one feels best):

- "Even though the tapping isn't working, I'm okay"
- "Even though I find it hard to get in touch with my emotions, I'm okay"
- "Even though I have shut myself down, I'm okay"
- "Even though I'm really scared of feeling my emotions, I'm okay"
- "Even though I'm scared of changing, I'm okay"

You may need to work with a therapist if you are really blocked.

If you are on antidepressants or other medication that might be blocking your emotions then the tapping may be less successful. I'd still use it though as it will work to some extent. In the long term the EFT can help you come off the antidepressants (with your doctor's approval of course) so it's worth persevering.

When to use EFT

The more you use EFT the more it will help. It can be used in two ways:

1. When you are feeling triggered by something in the moment.
2. For working at a deeper level to change your background thoughts, beliefs and traumas.

A good place to start is to get into the habit of tapping away negative thoughts and emotions every day as they arise in the moment. Just tap on exactly what you are feeling, for example "Even though I feel sad and upset/angry because..., I'm okay". Every time you get triggered by something or you realise you are feeling anxious or down then use it like a first aid remedy "Even though I'm having a really bad day today and am feeling really anxious, I'm okay".

➛ ***EFT does look a bit silly but you can do it in your bedroom, or take yourself off to the toilet if you are in a public place. You can also do it silently in your head and visualise yourself tapping (or just tap discretely on the Karate Chop point under the table and think the words).***

If you feel as if EFT is too difficult to do by yourself (we are all different and some people will definitely find it harder than others), then check out my website at www.eleanorhatherley.com/workshops. I am planning to do some teen tapping workshops and details of upcoming sessions and dates will be posted there.

CHAPTER 3

Working on your wallpaper

If you are still mastering the basics of EFT, you can come back to this chapter later.

Also, as we are all different, some of you might be finding EFT a bit too complicated. If this is you, then just ignore this chapter but do some simple tapping on any traumas, beliefs, fears and phobias. Here are some suggested phrases, but you can make your own up too:

- **Limiting beliefs** – "Even though I believe ... because ..., I'm okay"
- **Traumas** – "Even though I had this ... trauma and it made me feel ..., I'm okay"
- **Fears/phobias** – "Even though I am scared of ... because ... I'm okay"

Remember, the main purpose of EFT is to get in touch with the emotions behind the issue and by focusing on the issue, even at a surface level, it gives the body permission to let emotions come up. Just tap on and feel any emotions that come up. Or you can just sit with the emotions using the BAE technique.

If you are enjoying using EFT and you are happy to go a bit deeper with it, I am now going to share some techniques which will help you to clear some of your subconscious limiting beliefs, traumas, fears and phobias that are contained in your wallpaper.

Tapping on limiting beliefs

As we looked at earlier, your wallpaper will be full of limiting beliefs about yourself and the world. These will be coming from your subconscious mind and will be making you think and act in a way that isn't really you. It can be useful to do some tapping on these.

Start by making a list of some of your biggest limiting beliefs. Examples of limiting beliefs might include:

- I'm not ... (good enough, strong enough, powerful enough, clever enough, pretty enough, funny enough, loveable enough, popular enough, confident enough, etc).
- I'm too... (too loud, too big, too annoying, too clumsy, too sensitive, too stupid, too boring, etc).
- I'm really... (useless, slow, weird, different, indecisive, selfish, weak, ugly, horrible, unkind, mean, disgusting, etc).
- I'm scared of ... (illness, death, germs, emotions, other people, other people's emotions, bullies, teachers, parents, punishment, etc).

Pick out anything from this list that feel true. You can also look back at the list of common limiting beliefs in Box 1 on page 45 to see which ones you put ticks or stars against. Make a list of all the limiting beliefs that you find, with the ones that are affecting you most at the top.

Taking the top belief, follow these five steps. I am going to use the belief of not being loveable as an example, but just insert your own belief:

1. **Tap on the belief.** Just say exactly what you believe and how it feels for you right now. For example:
   - "Even though I believe that I am not loveable, I'm okay."
   - "Even though I believe that there is something wrong with me and I will never be loveable, I'm okay."
   - "Even though this belief about not feeling loveable is making my life difficult, I'm okay."

2. **Tap on when the belief was created.** You might not know this exactly but just tap on whatever comes up. Get in touch with any emotions too if you can. Here are a couple of suggestions:
    - "Even though I have never felt loveable, I'm okay."
    - "Even though I'm not sure why or when I formed the belief that I am not loveable, I'm okay."
    - "Even though I decided I'm not loveable when...... happened, I'm okay"
3. **Tap on what you know now that you didn't know then.** Look back with more grown up perspective and see if you can see it all differently. Is the belief really true? Tap on these kind of things:
    - "Even though I formed this belief that I'm not loveable, it was because I thought ...., I'm okay."
    - "Even though I have this belief that I'm not loveable, I now know that ...., I'm okay."
4. **Tap on letting the belief go.** Do you really want to hold on to this belief? Tap to help let it go. For example:
    - "Even though I have this belief that I'm not loveable, I'm open to the possibility that it's not true, I'm okay."
    - "Even though I have this belief that I'm not loveable, I'm ready to start letting it go so I can be happier, I'm okay."
5. **Tap on the opposite of the belief.** Tap slowly around, saying a positive affirmation ("I am loveable") or a universal affirmation ("I am love") at each tapping point. Take a slow breath in and out after you say the affirmation. You can also vary the wording. For example:
    - "I am just as loveable as everyone else."
    - "I have always been loveable but I didn't realise it."
    - "I've had enough of not feeling loveable, I'm done with it."

If you find yourself arguing with or disagreeing with any of these statements then just tap on whatever comes up. It's showing you that you still have the belief and the 'buts' will give you useful information.

Continue to work through your list of limiting beliefs in this way. Create a regular tapping habit – perhaps set aside some time each day. Work on one limiting belief a day, or one a week if it's a big one.

It can be difficult to clear beliefs down so keep persevering. Remember that your subconscious will need a lot of persuading! The more you tap the looser the beliefs will get. A belief that feels 100% true is going to have more impact on you than a belief that only feels 50% true.

And remember that we are all different. So when you are working with your beliefs be realistic about yourself. Some of your beliefs may actually be true (for example, you may well be louder than others, or less clever). What's important is how you feel about it.

The aim is to be happy with who you are and to turn your traits into a positive rather than a negative. So tap on these traits to change how you feel about yourself ("Even though I hate it that I'm louder than other people, I'm okay"). Then bring in something positive when you feel better about it ("Even though I loud, it's really useful because ...., I'm okay).

Clearing traumas

We looked at traumas in the first section and we learnt a seven-step process for starting to unpick these. EFT is a good way to work further on these traumas. A quick reminder first though:

➤ ***It's best not to work by yourself on any traumas which bring up very strong emotions, or any that you have blocked out and it feels like you just can't go there.***

If you do have any of these kind of traumas, you will need to work with an EFT therapist or other professional who will guide you through the process and support you through any feelings that might come up. Or you could ask one of your parents or another appropriate adult to help you.

EFT is great for working on your less overwhelming traumas. Look back through your life and see if you can find some defining moments when things changed for you. What happened? What went wrong for you?

Also, if anything really big has happened to you (being ill, your parents divorcing, someone dying, an accident etc) then these are good to tap on too. You may not realise how much they have affected you.

Also, what trauma did you work on in Exercise 4 on page 34? This will be something quite big as it's affecting your every day life.

Once you have found some traumas, write them down, putting them in order of how much you think they are affecting you. Cross any out that feel too big or scary to work on alone.

Now pick your top (safe) trauma and rate it out of 10 (0 being it doesn't affect you at all and 10 being it affects you all the time). If your score is 7 or higher, give your trauma a title (eg, 'Giving a Speech'). Then just tap on the title for a few rounds until it feels a bit calmer ("Even though I have this 'Giving a Speech' trauma, I'm okay"). Don't go into any detail, just keep tapping on the title. This helps to take some of the emotional charge out of it so it's more comfortable to work on. Try and get it below a 5.

Once your trauma feels calmer, ask yourself these questions and do a few rounds on each answer:

1. **What happened?** Tap on anything you remember about the trauma. If it's hard to get in touch with it, you can tell yourself the story of it.
2. **How did it make you feel?** Tap on how the trauma made you feel deep inside ("Even though I felt really overwhelmed, unsafe and exposed").
3. **What was the very worst thing about it?** Tap on the very worst thing about the trauma ("Even though I made a fool of myself").
4. **What was the shock?** Can you spot the moment when the shock landed? What the shock was actually about? Tap on that ("Even though I got a shock when I saw everyone looking at me").
5. **Which emotions did you feel?** Tap on any emotions that overwhelmed you during the trauma ("Fear, shame and embarrassment"). Really allow yourself to feel them. You can use the BAE technique too.
6. **Does your body need to do anything?** What do you need to do to release the trauma? You might need to cry or scream or run or flail your

arms around. Just allow it to happen without any judgement. You can do it all silently or in your mind if this is more comfortable.

7. **What sensations did you experience?** Ask yourself what you saw, heard, felt, smelt and tasted during the trauma. Tap on all of these as the body often stores traumas via the five senses.
8. **What limiting beliefs and vows did you form?** Ask yourself what limiting beliefs and vows you might have formed about yourself and the world as a result of this trauma. Do some tapping on these ("Even though I decided I was very sensitive", "Even though I decided never to stand out again").
9. **Can you reframe the trauma?** Ask yourself what you know now that you didn't know then. Tap on your new learnings ("Even though I know now that it doesn't really matter if I get things wrong").
10. **How will my life improve without this trauma?** What could your life be like now this trauma is not affecting you as much? Tap on all the things you can do or believe now ("Even though it's safe to be seen now").

Traumas can be difficult to clear and you may need to revisit them many times. This is because there may be many different ASPECTS to them. Aspects are like all the little details of the trauma, everything that happened and everything you felt. It's hard to clear the trauma unless all the aspects have been cleared. Each time you work on the trauma you will find more aspects.

See Box 9 on the next page for an example of a trauma and all its aspects – you can see how many little subtle aspects there are to this seemingly small trauma.

Working on named conditions with EFT

Some of you will be suffering with specific named conditions like depression, anxiety, phobias, OCD, anorexia, bulimia or body dysmorphia.

➤ ***I wanted to remind you that these conditions are not things that have 'happened' to you. They are symptoms of your subconscious thoughts, beliefs, feelings and poorly managed emotions. Because they have been***

BOX 9 Aspects of a trauma

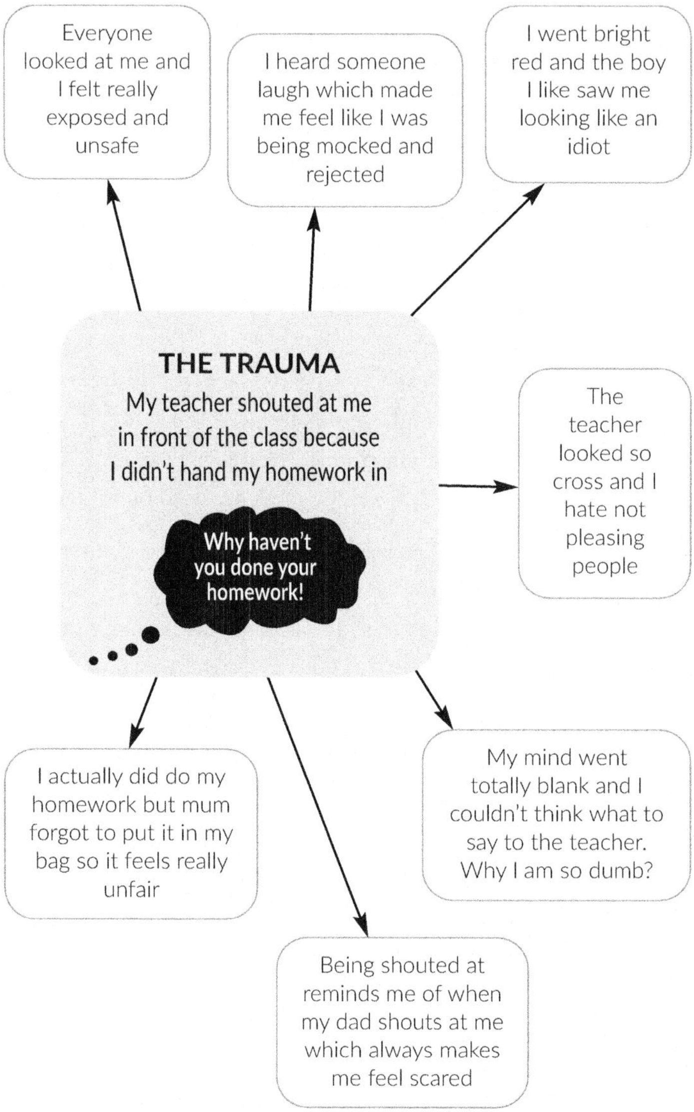

> ***given labels they seem more real but it is useful to try not to buy into the label too much as it just becomes a story that you live out of.***

EFT can be very helpful for getting to the root of these issues. A good place to start is by doing some tapping on how you feel about HAVING the issue. These feelings will actually be adding a lot to your issue. Imagine if you had the issue but didn't really mind. Wouldn't that feel easier?

Keep your set-up phrase simple. Here are some examples:

- "Even though I am scared of germs, I'm okay"
- "Even though I can't stop counting and checking, I'm okay"
- "Even though I hate my body, I'm okay"

Using these kind of statements will help to loosen it all up a bit. If it feels very overwhelming to be tapping on your issue then get some help with it rather than working on it alone.

These five steps will help you to understand why you might have your issue:

1. **What was going on in your life when it started?** You might immediately think of something big and obvious (ie, "After I had that big accident" or "When my dad left"). Or your answer might be more general (ie, "When I started secondary school"). If you get a more general answer, see if you can spot any particularly memorable moments or problems. Write down any traumas you find, big, small or ongoing.
2. **Is there anything going on in your wallpaper that could be contributing?** The symptoms you are having (the OCD, the phobia, the eating disorder) will be like the tip of the iceberg so dig down into your wallpaper and see what's lurking below. How do you feel about yourself, have you created any stories about yourself?
3. **What limiting beliefs are contributing to this condition?** Ask yourself what you mistakenly believe about yourself and life that is allowing you to keep holding on to this issue.
4. **What is this condition helping you to get, have, feel or avoid?** Sometimes we adopt a particular behaviour as it fills a hole (eg, we might overeat because we feel unloved and eating feels comforting).

A behaviour can also help us avoid something (eg, we might wash our hands a lot because we don't want to catch germs as we fear death).

5. **What emotions do I not want to feel and why?** This is very important. Many of these conditions are due to not wanting to feel overwhelming emotions. See if you can get a sense of the emotion you are scared of. Why are you scared of feeling it? Can you reconsider this now that you know more about emotions and have EFT to help you?

Tap on all your answers and any traumas and limiting beliefs that you find. Use the BAE technique for any repressed emotions.

It can be tough to clear some of these conditions, even with EFT. They may have formed from many separate events and beliefs and you might have to do a lot of unpicking. But it's a really useful process to go through as not only will it help to clear the issue but it will also help you to clear some core stuff in your wallpaper which will definitely be affecting you.

Section 8 explores all the common mental health issues and looks at what each issue could be showing you about yourself. You will find more information about your particular issue there.

Tapping directly on your wallpaper

As well as clearing traumas, limiting beliefs and specific conditions, it can also be useful to tap directly on these three core things:

1. Are you constantly trying to be like everyone else and focusing on where you think you lack rather than on who you really are?
2. Have you created any negative and untrue stories about yourself, based on your experiences during your childhood?
3. Do you love (or even like) yourself? If the answer is no, then why?

Spend a bit of time focusing on each of these as they are very important. Tap on anything that comes up and try and make some changes to all these untrue stories and perceptions about yourself. These three things, along with traumas, are often at the foundation of poor mental health.

SECTION 5

Building resilience

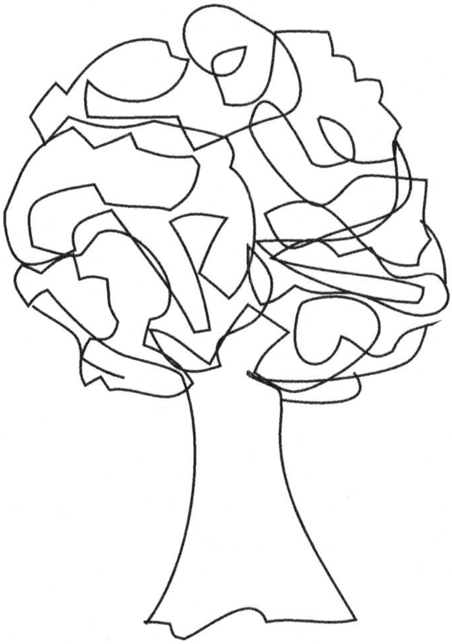

CHAPTER 1

The nervous system

In this section we are going to look at how we can improve our mental health by becoming more resilient. Let's start by defining 'resilient'.

Resilience

Resilient means feeling strong and powerful and not being too sensitive to or over alert to potential danger. If we have good resilience then we are able to cope much better with anything that life throws at us.

Some people are more resilient than others. They just tend to cope calmly and things don't affect them too much.

Other people are very sensitive and easily upset and the smallest thing can feel very overwhelming and difficult. Life then becomes a constant struggle, with a feeling that danger is always lurking just around the corner and that we won't be strong enough to cope with it.

So why do our levels of resilience vary so much? I believe there are four main reasons:

1. **Our character.** Because we are all different, some of us are more sensitive, creative and imaginative than others. This can affect our resilience because we tend to be more alert and aware of everything that is happening around us. We also create imaginative, complex and

often fearful 'what if' stories about the future in our minds and then live out of these stories as if they are true.

2. **Our wallpaper.** If we have a lot of limiting beliefs and perceptions about ourselves, we are not going to be as resilient as someone who is more positive. Resilient people usually believe they are strong and powerful and that life is safe. If you know a resilient person, ask them what they believe about themselves and see how it differs from what you believe.
3. **Developmental trauma.** When we are in the womb and during the first two years of our lives, our nervous system forms in response to what is happening to us. So, if your mother is very stressed while you are in the womb or you are born into a dangerous environment, your nervous system will form to be more sensitive and reactive. This would have been useful in the past as being more alert to danger would have kept us safer. But now life is pretty safe for most of us and this over sensitive nervous system can work against us.
4. **The freeze response.** When we are very young we lack perspective and don't have many resources so we feel small, weak and helpless. We therefore often respond to traumas or difficult things by freezing. Our nervous system then gets cluttered up with lots of unprocessed and frozen traumas which makes it more sensitive and reactive.

Of these four reasons, there isn't much we can do about our character except to learn to really be ourselves which will help us to feel safer and more powerful. And we have already looked at how you can change the beliefs in your wallpaper. We will look in more detail at developmental trauma and the freeze response in the next two chapters but, first, let's have a quick overview of the nervous system.

The nervous system

The nervous system is divided into two parts:

1. **The sympathetic nervous system.** When we think we are in danger, this prepares the body for stress. It makes the heart beat faster, sends blood

to the muscles, releases adrenaline, etc. It is known as the 'fight or flight' response.

2. **The parasympathetic nervous system.** This returns the body to rest, calming the heart and the stress chemicals. It also helps digestion, and the healing and repair of cells.

These two systems balance each other, a bit like an accelerator and a brake. If we experience danger, we go into a sympathetic (alert) state. Once the danger is over we go back to a parasympathetic (resting) state.

We should mainly be in the parasympathetic state, resting, absorbing food and repairing. The problem is many of us get stuck in a sympathetic state.

➤ ***Symptoms of being in a sympathetic state include things like anxiety, panic attacks, nervousness, breathlessness, palpitations, inability to relax, poor sleep, feeling jumpy or jittery and having poor digestion.***

Being stuck in this sympathetic state makes us less resilient as our nervous system is constantly on high alert for danger. It is a very unpleasant and unhealthy way to live and it won't make you happy.

So how can you get back to living in a more parasympathetic (resting) state so you can become more resilient?

As I said earlier in the chapter, you will need to look at your wallpaper and your limiting beliefs as this will help you to create a new and less fearful story about yourself and the world. This will help to calm your nervous system down.

Developmental trauma and the freeze response can also have a big impact on our nervous system and our resilience so let's have a look at each of these in the next two chapters.

First, have a look at Exercise 13 to see whether you are in a parasympathetic or sympathetic state.

EXERCISE 13 What state are you in?

Sit quietly, close your eyes and take a few deep and calming breaths. Come out of your thoughts and let your attention rest in your body.

What is going on in your body? Does it feel relaxed or are you on alert? What is your heart doing? How about your breathing? Is your stomach clenched or relaxed? Are there any other uncomfortable sensations in your body? Is your mind busy or still? Do you feel a sense of danger or is everything okay?

Now give yourself a score out of 10 for how stressed you feel, 0 being very relaxed and 10 being very stressed. If your body feels calm and relaxed and you gave yourself a low score, sit and enjoy this feeling of being in a parasympathetic state. Familiarise yourself with it so that you can come back to it when you are stressed.

If your body feels like it is on alert and you gave yourself a high score, just notice the sensations of being in a sympathetic state. Don't judge it, just sit with it and really feel it. Be aware that everything that is happening in your body is in response to your thoughts. Take a few calming breaths and keep focusing on your body and your breath. This will help to relax your mind and bring you back into a more parasympathetic state. Notice the sensations in your body changing as this happens.

Follow the actions below to help you be more parasympathetic.

Ongoing actions

- Repeat the above exercise whenever you need to calm yourself.
- Notice when you are in a sympathetic or parasympathetic state and see if you can spot what kind of things trigger each of these states.

CHAPTER 2

Developmental trauma

In this chapter we are going to look at how development trauma can affect the nervous system, priming us to spend more time in sympathetic (alert) mode.

Developmental trauma

From conception until around the age of two, our nervous system is still developing. This means that we can't regulate it ourselves and we rely on a parent or caregiver to comfort and soothe us and keep us feeling safe, loved and nourished so we can learn to do these things for ourselves.

If we don't get this feeling of safety then our nervous system will be wired to be more reactive to danger. It's a survival thing – if we are born into a dangerous environment then we need to be EXTRA responsive.

It can start in the womb. If your mother is very stressed during pregnancy, you will be bathed in a cocktail of stress hormones which will prime your nervous system to be more responsive to danger.

And sometimes during the first two years of our life we don't get the right sort of care. Perhaps your parents or caregivers have their own mental health issues or addiction issues, or perhaps there is other stuff going on like illness, hospital stays, divorce, being very busy, having to work long hours, or even having a lot of children to take care of.

➛ ***Whatever sort of parenting you have had, please don't blame your parents. It's not at all easy to be a parent and everyone is affected by the stuff in their wallpaper. Some parents will be struggling with their own poor mental health and this can make it difficult to take care of others.***

How does developmental trauma affect us?

There are three main ways that development trauma can show up:

1. Feeling very anxious, easily overstimulated and easily overwhelmed. Life feels scary and difficult and you will find it hard to self calm.
2. Finding it difficult to control your emotions and behaviour. This might include uncontrolled rage or other 'bad' behaviours which can get diagnosed as something like ADHD.
3. Becoming very shut down and frozen.

There are many levels of development trauma ranging from those who are so affected by it that they can barely function, down to those who have it at a very mild level which might give rise to occasional symptoms such as anxiety or not feeling safe.

Do you have developmental trauma?

Many of us probably have some degree of developmental trauma as it's very difficult for parents to give you everything you need all the time.

What was your early childhood like? Was there anything obvious going on like physical or mental abuse, violence, a lack of love or care, addictions, mental health issues, a messy divorce, illness, etc?

Also, what was your birth like? This is your first interaction with the world and it sets a standard. Was it stressful? Were there problems? Did you get separated from your mother when you were first born?

Even if there is nothing big and obvious in your early childhood, do you feel as if you got the love, care and protection you needed?

I just wanted to say again, please remember that it's not about blame. It's difficult being a human being and really none of us are very good at it.

Working with developmental trauma

When we are in the womb and very young we don't have access to words or to sophisticated thought processes. This means that everything would have been experienced as bodily sensations. The best way to work with developmental trauma is therefore through the body, really getting in touch with any repressed feelings of fear, unsafety, aloneness, being unsupported, sadness, overwhelm, etc.

If you have been really affected by developmental trauma then you will need to get professional help to do this. There are therapists who specialise in developmental trauma (ie, somatic therapy) but you could also try an EFT therapist. See www.eleanorhatherley.com/therapy-info.

If you had a generally okay or good childhood but have a feeling of not being safe and connected, then you can try doing some simple tapping on these feelings, or you can use the BAE technique.

It is also helpful to regularly do things that help you relax as this will teach your nervous system a new way of being. We will look at this in more detail in Chapter 4.

Now let's have a look at Exercise 14 to help you dial down your nervous system a bit.

EXERCISE 14 Dialling down

Sit quietly, close your eyes and take a few deep and calming breaths. We are going to get in touch with your nervous system.

Don't overthink it. Imagine it like a humming sensory energy in and around you. Get a sense of whether it's running fast. Is it full of fear? Whatever comes up, just sit with the feelings for a few moment, fully allowing and accepting all sensations and feelings. Don't worry if you can't feel anything, just guess how it might feel.

Now I want you to imagine a big dial which you can turn up or down. If your nervous system feels too responsive, turn the dial down a bit. Or, if you feel disconnected and shut down then you might want to turn the dial up a bit. Don't go too high – it is better for your body and your mental health to have a calm nervous system.

Once you have got the dial exactly at the right setting, see if this new feeling has a colour. Perhaps something like pale blue, pink, green, yellow or white? See what feels right to you. Spend a few minutes breathing this colour into your body and deep into your nervous system. Don't worry if you can't see a colour, just breathe.

Follow the ongoing actions below to help you soothe your nervous system so that you feel safer and more connected.

Ongoing actions

- Repeat the above exercise whenever you feel stressed.
- Get professional help if you feel as if you have been really affected by developmental trauma.
- If you had a generally good childhood then use EFT or the BAE technique to work on any bodily feelings of unsafety, overwhelm or shut down.

CHAPTER 3

The freeze response

As well as being affected by developmental trauma, our nervous system can be affected by the freeze response. Let's have a look at this in more detail.

The freeze response

We have evolved from reptiles to mammals and then to human beings. This means that our brain has three different layers and each of these three layers has a different way of coping with danger:

1. The human (rational) brain tries to think it away or to manage it using language and other intelligent strategies.
2. The animal (emotional) brain makes us run away or fight.
3. The reptilian (instinctual) brain make us freeze.

When you experience danger, your brain works out which strategy is best, moving down through these layers. It might try reasoning or talking it away and, if this doesn't work, it'll try running away or fighting. If this isn't going to work either then the only thing left to do is to freeze.

Freezing is all about overwhelm. You are so terrified that you dissociate from your body so that you can't feel what is about to happen to you. It's like you are making yourself disappear, or surrendering to death. It can be a good strategy in an ACTUAL survival situation as it numbs us to pain and shuts down our emotions temporarily.

➤ ***For an animal it can also work well as a predator might not be able to see them if they stop moving.***

When we are very young we often react to traumas by going straight into this freeze response. This is because we don't have the resources to reason, run or fight. We feel small, defenceless and weak and are easily overwhelmed.

These types of traumas can really create a problem for our nervous systems. Let's look at why.

Releasing the freeze response

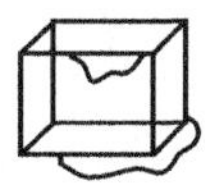

The freeze response can be very useful but we are supposed to release it once the danger has passed.

Animals do this quickly and easily. If a deer is being chased by a lion, it runs as fast as it can and kicks out at the lion. When the lion is very close to catching the deer it will freeze (it's tried running and the kicking didn't work so there's no other option). It's then either caught and eaten (game over) or it gets away (perhaps the lion can't see it any more). If it escapes, once the danger is over it will discharge the freeze response.

Now imagine that at the moment it freezes a snapshot is taken of how it's feeling and what it's doing. When it discharges the freeze it goes back to this exact moment to complete it. It will run and kick up its hooves and it will tremble and shake to get rid of any excess adrenaline. Then it will return to a relaxed state.

To release the freeze as humans, we also need to go back to how we were feeling when we went into the freeze. So we would need to re-experience the emotions we were feeling and we might also need to act them out physically – perhaps by crying, screaming, punching, kicking, running – to really let them go. This helps to discharges the freeze and we can go back to normal relaxed behaviour.

How the freeze response goes wrong for us

The problem is that our thinking human brains get in the way. Many of us are scared of feeling strong emotions and will avoid doing so at all costs. We particularly don't want to feel the emotions from a trauma as they remind us of how we felt and it doesn't feel safe to ever feel that way again.

We also wouldn't feel comfortable flailing around, kicking, punching and screaming. We wouldn't know we were releasing the freeze response and we'd probably think we were going MAD! So we'd push the emotions down and stop ourselves. This then stops us from discharging the freeze.

And when we don't release the freeze response, it gets trapped in our body and this disrupts our nervous system. It goes onto high alert, always looking out for similar danger. Every time something happens that reminds you of the trauma, the repressed emotions will try and come up. And, as you won't feel comfortable with feeling them, you will push them down again.

➤ ***So not only will your nervous system be on high alert but you will also constantly be experiencing uncomfortable feelings from the trauma.***

Have a look at Box 10. This shows more visually how the freeze response gets interrupted and goes wrong for us.

I suspect that some of our mental health symptoms are our bodies trying to discharge these freeze responses. Imagine a situation where you were really frightened and you felt really panicked. You then go into freeze. Once you feel relaxed and safe again (and this can take hours, days, weeks, months, years or even decades) the body tries to discharge the freeze and you will suddenly feel panicked again. You'd then think "OMG, I'm having a panic attack completely out of nowhere while I'm relaxing on the sofa! There's something REALLY wrong with me!". It would be terrifying. And you'd fear it happening again, which could create a whole new trauma!

Another problem is that danger to us is not just a quick and defined experience like it was for the deer. We have complex minds and fearful imaginations and so we often feel as if we are in danger when we are not.

BOX 10 How the freeze response goes wrong

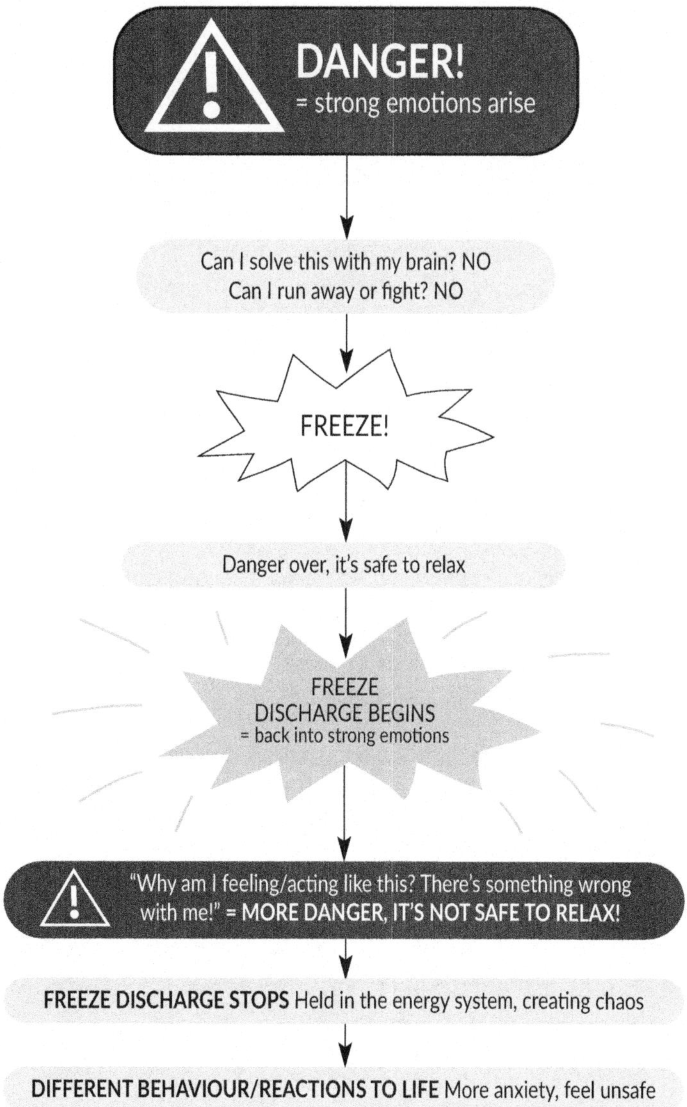

This means that it can be hard to get out of the freeze response as we don't ever really feel as if the danger is really gone and it's safe to release it.

Clearing the freeze response

Do you think that you might have been affected by this freeze response?

It can be difficult to remember traumas that happened to us when we were very young so it's easier to spot them through our reactions and bodily symptoms. What state is your nervous system in? Does part of you feel stuck and frozen? Are you always anxious and on edge? Do you get triggered? Do you struggle with certain emotions? Does life feel really unsafe? Do you sometimes get weird symptoms out of the blue when you relax? All of these can be a sign that you might have frozen traumas.

If you think you have a lot of frozen trauma that is really affecting you, you will have to get some professional help from a therapist who specialises in trauma. Somatic therapy is good or you could try an EFT therapist. See www.eleanorhatherley.com/therapy-info for more details.

If you just have a general sense that you might have some frozen trauma but that it's not too bad, then you can do some simple EFT on yourself. Remember, you need to work with your bodily sensations as these feelings are pre-verbal. The BAE technique is useful too. Really feel the frozen emotions and allow your body to express itself as it needs to.

➛ ***Just know that the things that overwhelmed you then probably wouldn't be a big deal now (unless it was something really massive in which case don't work on it alone). You have much better coping strategies and a lot more perspective. All that is going to happen is that you are going to feel some emotions. You know you can do that as we've already practiced doing it. You also have EFT which helps to calm strong emotions down. So you are older, stronger, wiser, and you have good tools and resources!***

Now let's look at Exercise 15 to see if you can get in touch with a frozen part of yourself.

EXERCISE 15 Unfreezing yourself

Sit quietly, close your eyes and take a few deep and calming breaths.

We are going to see if you can get in touch with a sense of a younger version of you who feels overwhelmed and scared. The trick is to not overthink it, but just allow it to pop up into your mind.

If you manage to connect with them, see how they are feeling. You can try asking them, or perhaps you just get a feeling in your body. It might be a sense of overwhelm, or fear, or aloneness. Just sit with whatever comes up, without any judgement. Fully accept any feelings and allow them to fill your body.

As you do this, visualise your younger self running around (a bit like the deer), discharging all the energy from the freeze. Let them do exactly what they need to do.

Now see how your younger self feels. They may feel better, or it may feel as if there's more to do. If there's more, carry on feeling the feelings and allowing your younger self to discharge the energy. Repeat this until they feel calmer and happier.

If you find this exercise difficult, don't worry. Try it again another time as it can get easier with practice. Some people find this kind of visualising very hard so don't worry if it's not for you.

Follow the ongoing actions below to help release frozen traumas.

Ongoing actions

- Repeat this exercise as many times as you want. It will help to let go of the overwhelm from old frozen traumas.
- Seek help if you are stuck in a big freeze response or, for smaller traumas, do some simple tapping and use the BAE technique.

CHAPTER 4

Creating relaxation

In the last two chapters we looked at developmental trauma and the freeze response. These both affect the state of the nervous system and mean that you spend too much time in a sympathetic (alert) state.

It can be difficult to really let these type of traumas go as they are embedded deep in our subconscious. As I said, you would need to work with a therapist if you are being really affected by this kind of trauma.

It is also important to keep working on your wallpaper as this is what feeds the subconscious mind. By making your beliefs and perceptions more positive, your mind and body will start to relax more.

Another way of moving into a more parasympathetic (resting) state is to teach your nervous system how to be more relaxed. There are many ways of doing this but the underlying message is practice, practice, practice. Remember, repetition is the ONLY way to change the subconscious mind, and this is where the roots of these nervous system behaviours lie.

Learning to relax

When I was a child, there wasn't much to do. You could watch TV but as there were only three channels it wasn't very exciting. Or you could listen to the radio or to music, or read a book. And that was about it for entertainment. The rest of the time you did stuff like drawing and painting, going out on your bike or spending time with friends. It meant that we were often bored and we'd lounge around the house in a bit of a vacant state, slightly switched off. This probably sounds terrible but it was actually very good for us.

Your generation has endless stimulating entertainment. You probably rarely feel bored. That's a good thing in some ways but it also means that your mind is constantly switched on. And your body will be responding to whatever your mind is doing. So whether you are playing a video game or scrolling through social media, your body will be a bit stressed (because it doesn't know the difference between real and imaginary danger).

And even if you are not always entertaining yourself on devices, perhaps you just have a really busy mind and find it hard to turn it off?

➤ ***This is me. I can go for a peaceful walk in the park and be stuck in my head the whole way round, thinking about all my problems.***

Whether we are over entertaining ourselves or just over thinking, being constantly switched on like this is not good for us. It's really important to have some time each day to empty your mind and relax your body. This will really help your nervous system to become more relaxed and resilient.

Meditation

Meditation is a good way to train the mind so that you can feel calmer and more in control of your thoughts. The ultimate aim during meditation is to go into a place of complete peace. However, it's also useful just at a basic level so don't put pressure on yourself to do it perfectly.

Meditation has many benefits and can really improve your mental health:

- It lowers your heart rate and slows down your breathing
- It lowers stress hormones
- It creates feelings of well being
- It allows you to relax more deeply
- It reduces anxiety and depression

Meditation can be difficult to do, especially if you have a very active mind, but the more you practice the easier it gets and the more it helps.

The best place to start is by focusing on one simple and calming thing. This helps to stop the mind drifting off into other thoughts. Here are some ideas for simple focused meditations:

- **Breathing meditation.** Become aware of your breathing. How does your body move as you breathe? Is your chest or stomach moving? Now breathe in through your nose and out through your mouth and slow the breathing down. Focus on the air coming into your nose and on the sound it makes as you let it out. Do this for a few minutes. Then, continuing to breathe in the same way, put your hand below your belly button and take ten slow breaths, filling your belly up. Finally, become aware of the end of each out breath and leave a short gap before you take the next breath in. For the next ten breaths, connect with the sense of stillness that is in this small gap. You can make the gap slightly longer if it feels comfortable to do this.
- **Candle meditation.** Light a candle and place it in front of you. Then just focus on the flame, staring at it with a soft and relaxed gaze. Don't worry if thoughts come in, just keep focusing on the flame. You can also do this with an open fire if you have one.
- **Bubble visualisation.** Sit quietly with your eyes closed. Each time you have a thought see it in a bubble floating up from your head. As the bubble moves away, see it popping. Repeat this with every thought.
- **Visualisation.** Sit quietly with your eyes closed. Imagine that you are in a relaxing and beautiful place. Really imagine you are there. What can you see and hear around you?
- **Positive affirmations.** Sit quietly with your eyes closed. Now think of all the negative stuff you believe about yourself and change it into the opposite. So, for example, if you feel weak, say "I am powerful". If your mind argues with it, then change it to "I am power". This gets you in touch with a more universal power rather than your own (which probably feels small and limited). Say the words and then see if you can

feel the power coming into you. Repeat this for any other negative beliefs.

Why not try each meditation and see which one works best for you? Some of us are better with visual things, some with sounds and some with sensations. Start by meditating for just a few minutes every day. Choose a time when you feel calm and a bit tired as it's easier to relax then.

Remember that it takes PRACTICE. The more you do it, the more your brain builds up the neural pathways and the easier it will get. Start with five minutes and then build it up. If you are really enjoying it then you can stretch it to 15 or even 30 minutes.

➣ ***Try and find little opportunities during the day to switch off and meditate. For example if you are on a car journey. You could also do a couple of minutes every time you go to bed and wake up in the morning.***

Once you feel more confident with meditation, there are lots of free meditations online. Check out the Resources section of my website for some links at www.eleanorhatherley.com/other-resources.

When meditation feels difficult

Some people really struggle with meditation. This is usually because they find it hard to switch off their thoughts.

If this is you, don't beat yourself up. We are all different and some of us have very strong and active minds which means that meditation is harder. Unfortunately, the harder your find it, the more you need to do it!

➣ ***I have an active mind and I found it really, really hard at first and got quite grumpy about doing it. I kept going though and now, as long as I do it at a time of day when I feel a bit tired, I really enjoy it.***

Start by just sitting with the feeling of discomfort. Just notice your busy thoughts and don't have any judgement about them. Keep returning to the meditation and don't have any expectations for how it should go. Just sitting quietly with your eyes closed is actually quite relaxing in itself.

Some people struggle with doing meditation because it doesn't feel safe to sit quietly. If this is you, you are probably the sort of person who likes to keep yourself busy and are constantly find things to absorb your mind so you never have to be aware of how you are feeling.

There are two reasons why meditation might not feel safe:

1. Your nervous system is in such a hyper state that it's telling you that it's not safe to relax.
2. You are repressing strong emotions or a trauma and it feels as if these might come up to the surface if you let go and relax.

The best way to deal with either of these is to start by doing a very simple meditation. As soon as you start feeling anxious or uncomfortable then STOP and move around to discharge the energy. Then try the meditation again. This time, allow the feelings to come up for a little longer. Just sit with them and feel their full intensity. Each time you feel uncomfortable or overwhelmed, stand up and move around again. Then try again.

It's a bit like doing the BAE technique. You are just letting strong feelings and emotions fully in before you can let them go. Just sit with any feelings of discomfort and resistance and allow the full intensity to fill your body without judgement. You will probably find it easier to meditate next time but, if not, then just repeat the above steps. You are actually doing lots of important work on yourself.

If you are still struggling to meditate, do some tapping on it. See what is behind it. By clearing some of the deeper stuff, it makes it easier to relax.

Being in the present moment

Most of the time we are thinking about things that have happened in the past or we are focusing on how we think the future is going to be.

But we can't change the past and we don't really know how the future is going to be. We think we are staying in control by thinking out every little detail about the future but it's an illusion as we don't really have much control over how life unfolds. We actually just create a lot of anxiety by trying to control the future.

Next time you feel anxious, ask yourself whether there is any actual REAL danger or whether you are just making up a story about the future.

➤ ***It's very hard to predict the future and we nearly always get it wrong. The things we worry about rarely happen and the things that DO happen are often completely unexpected.***

Actually neither the past or the future really exist. All there is is the present moment. Learning to be more in the present moment is one of the most important things we can do to improve our mental health. It does take a bit of practice, but is worth the effort as it helps us to stop obsessing over the past or fearing the future.

To stay in the present moment we have to be 'mindful'. We have to really concentrate on our senses (sight, sound, touch, taste and smell) and to slow ourselves right down so we can absorb every detail. This is known as 'mindfulness'.

Here are a few ways to practice mindfulness:

- **Mindful eating.** Get a piece of fruit or chocolate (or something else that you like) and have a really good look at it. What can you see? What colour and texture is it? What about the shape? How does it feel on your skin? How does it smell? How does the smell make you feel? Now touch it to your tongue and see how it tastes. Then bite a small piece off and chew it very slowly. Hold it in your mouth and really savour it. Repeat this for each mouthful until you have finished it.
- **Mindful movement.** Walk slowly around your room and really notice how your body moves. Start with your toes. What happens to them each time you take a step? What are the sensations? Then move to the ball of your foot, then your heel, then your ankle, moving up your whole body very slowly, repeating this enquiry each time.
- **Mindful walking.** Go for a walk and really be aware of your surroundings. What can you see? What can you hear? What can you

smell? How does the air feel on your skin? Really notice every little detail.

You can apply mindfulness to EVERYTHING. For example, eating a meal, tidying your room, having a shower, putting makeup on. Get creative with it and practice it as often as you can. Remember to always get in touch with your senses (sight, sound, smell, touch and taste).

Once you have mastered mindfulness it's a very useful technique for when you are feeling stressed as it gets you out of your thoughts.

Breathing techniques

Breathing is another very good way of calming the mind and the body down. The more anxious we feel, the faster and shallower our breathing gets. This sends a feedback loop to your mind saying that there is danger and it increases the feeling of stress in the mind.

It's good to be aware of your breathing. The correct way to breathe is into your belly. So when you take a breath in, your belly fills up and sticks out slightly. And when you breathe out it goes back down again. Some people breathe back to front and suck their belly in when they breathe in. If this is you, you need to work on changing this as it affects your mental state.

➤ ***Another bad habit we get into is to breathe in a shallow way so that the breath is only in our chest. This will make your breathing restricted and tight and will again signal danger to your mind. Shallow breathing tends to happen more when we are stressed.***

So the first thing to do is to notice your breathing over a couple of days. Start by seeing what it's like when you are resting and relaxed. What speed does it go? Are you breathing into your belly or chest? If you are breathing very fast or are not breathing deeply into your belly, then spend some working on this. Put your hand under your belly button and breathe down into your hand with long steady breaths.

Also observe what happens to your breathing when you are feeling stressed. Does it get tight and shallow? Is it jerky? Make a conscious effort to slow it down and expand it back into your belly. Again, this will take practice but the more you do it the easier it will get. Focusing on your breathing will also take you out of your thoughts so it will help you feel less mentally engaged with the thing that is stressing you.

There are lots of breathing exercises online. I like the 4-7-8 technique. It really calms the whole nervous system down and helps train your body to breathe deeper and slower. It's a useful technique for helping you deal with stress. Here's how to do it:

1. Breathe out slowly and completely through your mouth, making a soft 'whoosh' sound.
2. Close your mouth and breathe in quietly and slowly through your nose while silently counting to four.
3. Hold your breath for a count of seven.
4. Breathe out completely through your mouth, making a 'whoosh' sound to a count of eight.
5. Now repeat steps 2 to 4 three more times.

You can also use the gap technique that we used in the breathing meditation earlier in this chapter. Get your breathing into a good rhythm and then focus on the end of the out breath. Leave a small gap before you breathe in again. Focus on the stillness in this gap and increase the length of it if you can. Then try and expand this sense of stillness that is in the gap into the whole breath and your whole body.

Building future resilience

In addition to meditation, mindfulness and breathing, there are lots of other ways to calm your nervous system down and to improve your resilience. Here is a list of ideas. Try and do as many of them as much as possible so that you wire in some new habits and ways of being:

- **Acupuncture.** Acupuncture helps to calm and balance your body. It is based on the idea that there are five different types of energy in your body and if one of these is out of balance it can cause a range of problems, including stress and depression. Acupuncturists use very fine needles to help rebalance you and, as it has been found to be scientifically effective, doctors will now often recommend it.

- **Exercise.** Physical activities such as singing, dancing or playing an instrument are all good ways to relax. Try some of these out and see which ones work for you. You can join a class or do it on your own. Just make sure you enjoy it and really engage with it.
- **Burn it off.** If your nervous system is in sympathetic alert mode a lot, find a physical outlet for your fight or flight energy (kick boxing, running, football, going to the gym, etc).
- **Calming activities.** Spend every day doing something calming to soothe your nervous system. Perhaps spending time with a pet, listening to soothing music, reading a calming book, baking, drawing or painting.
- **Community.** Being part of a supportive community makes us feel more resilient. Is there someone in your family you can talk to about problems? Or perhaps a family friend or another relative? If you don't have the right people around you, is there a group you could join?
- **Beliefs.** Have a look at your limiting beliefs and see if they are adding to your lack of resilience. Perhaps you believe you are weak, helpless, easily overwhelmed, too sensitive? Do some tapping on this and see if you can work out why you believe these things about yourself.
- **Affirmations.** Use universal affirmations regularly to help you feel more strong and powerful (ie, "I am power", "I am resilience").
- **Positive EFT.** Use positive EFT regularly on yourself (see page 99) so you can start getting in touch with some of the qualities you think you lack. This will help you to feel stronger, happier, calmer, etc.
- **Emotions.** Clear down any repressed emotions and learn to express emotions fully in the moment whenever they arise. Your nervous system will feel calmer if it's not clogged up with lots of emotion.
- **Acceptance.** Learn to not resist things. You can't change what is happening but you can change your reaction to it. Go with the flow. Practice the BAE technique on anything that feels overwhelming.

- **Be present.** Stay in the present moment and don't create fearful imaginary stories about the future. The future does not exist yet. Try and catch yourself doing this and make up a better story to live out of.
- **Love yourself.** Focus on being really kind to yourself. The more hard and judgmental you are, the more stressed you will be. Make it a project to be really kind and understanding. Love yourself. Stop focusing on where you think you lack and learn to really accept who you are.
- **Have fun.** Do things you love doing as often as possible and spend time with people who make you feel good. This will calm the nervous system.

Now let's complete Exercise 16 to help you to switch your mind off.

EXERCISE 16 Staying present

Sit quietly and close your eyes. Take a few deep and calming breaths.

Now imagine you have a timeline, starting from when you were in the womb and stretching into the future. I see my timeline in front of me, going from left to right with the past on my left and the future on my right. See what yours looks like. The past might be behind you and the future in front of you. Or it might be to the side like mine, or more diagonal or a mixture of any of these.

When you have a clear view of your timeline, look back and see yourself in the womb. Then move along it and see yourself getting older until you reach the present day. Then see the future stretched out. Perhaps you can see some things in your future timeline – an exam you are dreading, or something you are worrying about?

Then come back to where you are right now on your timeline. We are going to create a present moment channel. Imagine it like a wide channel that contains your body and goes up into space. It is very spacious and still and there is no sense of time. Your past and your future suddenly don't feel so important and your mind will probably be quieter. Sit with this for a few minutes and really connect.

Follow the ongoing actions below to help you build your resilience.

Ongoing actions

→ Repeat the above exercise regularly to help you be in the present moment.

→ Practice some meditation, mindfulness and breathing every day. Build them up gradually and use them when you feel stressed.

→ Regularly revisit the list of ways to build resilience so that you can start wiring in some new habits for the future.

SECTION 6

Self development

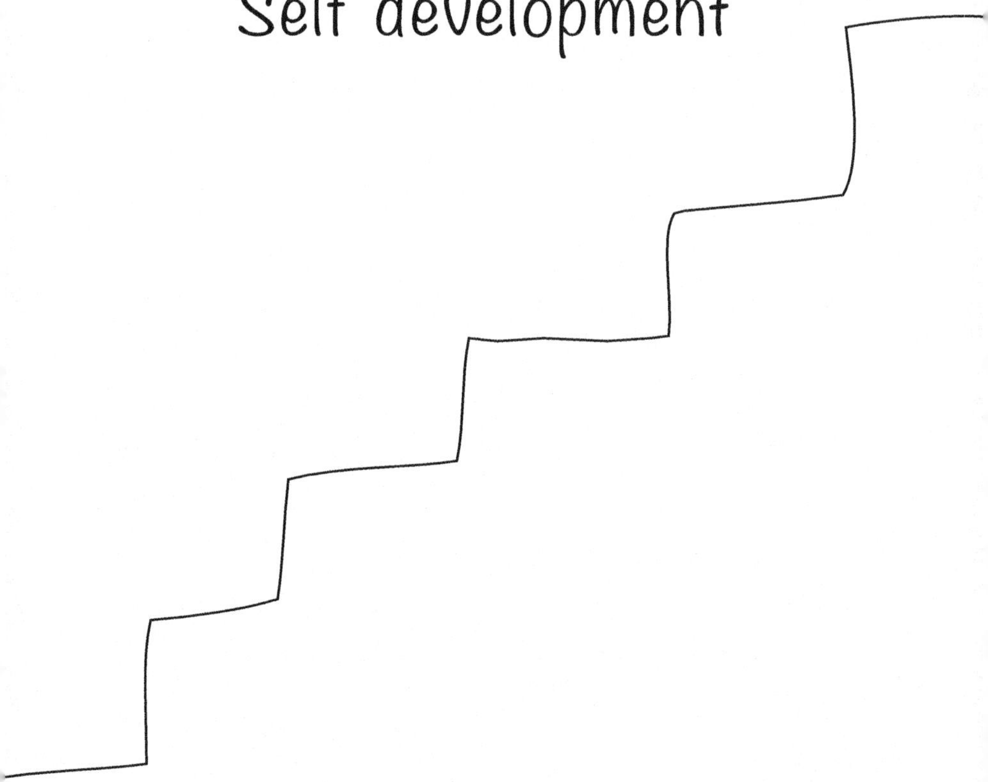

Yes NO NO Yes
Yes NO Yes NO

CHAPTER 1

Controlling your thoughts

In this section, we are going to look at some useful self development concepts which will help you to change the way you deal with yourself and with life. The more you can apply these the better.

In this first chapter we are going to look at the importance of learning how to control your thoughts.

Negative thinking

Negativity has an almost addictive energy to it and it's easy to keep returning to it. It's like picking a spot or scratching a sore. We know we shouldn't but it can almost be a like a compulsion.

It's easy to get stuck in a pattern of constantly complaining and criticising, focusing on all the things we haven't got or that we think are wrong with us or our lives. This makes us more and more negative and then more and more unhappy.

➤ ***The more unhappy we get, the more we complain and feel negative. This makes us even more unhappy so it's a vicious circle.***

We are naturally wired to think obsessively when we feel stressed as it helps us to solve problems. But most of the problems we face these days are PSYCHOLOGICAL rather than real (worries about looks, abilities, performance, fear of the future, etc). If your perception about yourself and the world is faulty (because of your limiting beliefs and untrue stories) then it will constantly seem as if there are lots of problems to stress over.

The best way to change this is to change your subconscious limiting beliefs and untrue stories. However, as this can be difficult and takes time, it's also good to learn how to control your conscious thoughts.

So how do we do this?

Controlling your conscious mind

Your mind probably feels as if it's very strong and domineering and that it just does its own thing. As I've already said, much of the mind is controlled by the subconscious and we really don't have much control over this part of it.

But we DO all have the ability to control our CONSCIOUS thoughts. We can choose to stop thinking about something negative and redirect our thoughts to something more positive. Remember the idea of the conscious mind being like a spotlight – you can choose where to put your attention. To do this, you have to watch yourself like a hawk. It takes practice but it's well worth doing.

Follow these three steps to help you start controlling your thoughts:

1. **Remind yourself that many of your thoughts are untrue.** You are running a script from a whole untrue story you have created about yourself and the world. Every thought and feeling you have in the present moment is connected to all your experiences in the past. It's very difficult to see things clearly as you will always be looking through a filter of your conditioning and past events. It's useful to remind yourself of this regularly. Use a sentence like "There are many ways to see things", or "I am only seeing things from my view", or "I can learn to see things differently". Find something that works for you.
2. **Practice noticing your thoughts.** Spend a day keeping a close watch on your thoughts. What kind of things take your attention? How many of

your thoughts are negative? How is your body feeling when you are thinking negative and fearful thoughts? Are your thoughts really serving you? If you find it hard to keep track of your thoughts then try keeping a journal. Write in it every day, just allowing your thoughts to flow onto the page. You can then read them back to see what is going on.

3. **Choose what you focus on.** Once you start to notice your negative thoughts, practice focusing on something more positive instead. Just say 'no' to yourself every time you notice you are thinking about something negative and then focus on something more positive. It can be something really small like the sound of a bird singing, or a beautiful colour, or something you are grateful for. It will feel a bit weird at first and your mind will definitely try to drag you back into its more familiar negativity so you will need to keep practising.

   ➤ ***Remember that every time you are thinking about something negative, you are reinforcing and strengthening all those faulty subconscious thoughts.***

When it feels difficult

Some people find it very difficult to control their conscious thoughts. This is probably because there is a lot of fearful and negative stuff going on in the subconscious mind and this can hijack the conscious mind.

If you are struggling, here are some suggestions for ways to calm and to switch off your negative thoughts:

1. **Distract your mind.** Find an activity where you have to concentrate on something else. This will stop your mind worrying away at all its problems. Try something like reading, gaming, watching a film, doing some homework, talking to friends, etc.
2. **Get into your body.** Anything that gets you out of your head and into your body will calm your mind. Go for a walk or do some exercise. Or connect with your senses – what can you see, hear, smell, feel and taste?
3. **Use universal affirmations (see Box 2 on page 47).** Your subconscious mind is a bit stupid and will believe anything you tell it, so try telling it

something really positive. If you are feeling powerless then say "I am power", "I am strength". If you are feeling unloved then try "I am love". Get creative with these affirmations and see how many you can think of. It will also give your mind something to focus on.

4. **Be grateful.** Focus on all the good things in your life. There will be lots of things, even if it doesn't feel as if there is. Make a list of as many things as you can think of. This will distract you from your negative thoughts and will make you feel lighter and happier.
5. **Meditation or mindfulness.** Meditation can really help to calm your mind down. If you have a really busy mind then it is good to meditate every day. You can also practice mindfulness to help you stay in the present moment. Go for a mindful walk or do something mindfully like taking a shower.
6. **Do the BAE technique.** When you feel really overwhelmed with negative thoughts, do the BAE technique. Sit quietly and observe your thoughts like a voice in your head. Let this voice shout and scream and totally express itself. Allow it to discharge all the energy and emotions that are behind the thoughts. Just sit calmly and watch. Don't have any judgement about what is happening. This will help to calm your thoughts down. Often they just need to be heard.
7. **Do some tapping.** If your thoughts feel really stuck in a big and charged negative story, do some simple tapping to acknowledge what you are thinking about and feeling. Really tap the emotion out of the thoughts. This will help to calm your mind down and let your thoughts go.

Work out the best way of changing YOUR thoughts and making them more positive. What takes you out of yourself? What distracts you? What makes you feel happy? Write a list of things and then when you feel overwhelmed by negative thoughts, use something on the list to take your focus elsewhere.

Now let's look at Exercise 17 to practise letting your thoughts go.

EXERCISE 17 Letting go of thoughts

Sit quietly and close your eyes. Just become aware of any thoughts, watching them for a few minutes. Don't try and stop them or change them. Be totally accepting of whatever is going on in your mind.

See if you can get a sense that you are standing back and watching your thoughts in the same way that you watch a film. Just allow them to scurry around in your head while you observe them. Let them do whatever they need to do. You can try imagining them like a ping pong ball bouncing around in your skull. Let the energy build up and go a bit crazy so all the energy gets released.

When your mind feels calmer, open your eyes and look around the room. Focus on each thing you see, really taking in the shape, the colour and the texture. Take your time over it and get a sense that there is plenty of time and space. Make sure your breathing is relaxed and deep as you look around.

How does your mind feel now? Hopefully a bit emptier and calmer?

Follow the ongoing actions below to help you get more control over your thoughts.

Ongoing actions

- Do the above exercise whenever your thoughts get out of control.
- Remind yourself that your thoughts are just a big story that you've made up and that you live out of.
- Practice noticing your thoughts and saying 'no' to negativity.
- Look for positive things to focus on, even really small things.
- Use distraction techniques when your mind is really negative.
- Tap on your negative thoughts to help clear your wallpaper.

CHAPTER 2

Blaming and shaming

Another area where we can make a change is to stop blaming others for our negative feelings and emotions.

Taking responsibility for our emotions

It's easy to blame others when we feel upset or angry. For example,
"My dad MAKES ME FEEL really angry when he tells me off",
"Mum MAKES ME FEEL really upset when she takes my brother's side",
"The popular girls at school MAKE ME FEEL really useless".

➤ ***When my daughter was little and we were out on a walk, she was being really slow, stopping to look at everything. I was feeling impatient and said to her "Hurry up, you are making me feel really stressed when you go so slowly" and she said "No, you're making yourself feel stressed". She was right, and very wise.***

We have to take responsibility for and ownership of our own emotions, even if it feels as if someone else is 'making' you feel something. No-one else can make you do or feel anything and what they are actually doing is triggering something in your wallpaper. So these feelings are actually showing you where your thoughts and beliefs are skewed. It's much easier to just feel angry or upset at the other person for disturbing your peace than it is to acknowledge that it's really coming from you.

So, taking the above examples, here are a few different scenarios for what might REALLY be going on below your surface reaction:

- **"My dad makes me feel really angry when he tells me off"**
  1. When he tells you off it makes you feel bad about yourself. You already feel down on yourself because of lots of stuff in your wallpaper and him telling you off makes you feel even worse.
  2. It feels unfair when he tells you off. Perhaps he once told you off really unfairly and this is an unresolved small trauma so it gets triggered every time you get told off?
- **"Mum makes me feel really upset when she takes my brother's side"**
  1. It makes you feel as if she loves him more than she loves you. You probably have some underlying issues around how loveable you are and you don't love yourself very much.
  2. You feel as if your mum didn't listen to your side of the argument properly. You might have some issues around being heard and understood which could come from a small trauma or it could be that you don't feel understood or powerful or important.
- **"The popular girls at school make me feel really useless"**
  1. You are already feeling useless about yourself and seeing these happy, popular girls makes you even more aware of your lack.
  2. You would really like to be part of the popular girls' group but because you are not you feel a bit useless and unimportant.

Can you see how there's so much information about you and your wallpaper behind these reactions? Next time someone else makes you feel angry or hurt, ask yourself what is REALLY going on. You might need to dig deep.

You might find that you are constantly getting triggered by the same thing or the same person. This is good to spot because it's showing you there's a big pattern in yourself that needs to be looked at. Make sure you do some work on it to change it. Staying constantly angry or upset at someone else only makes YOU suffer in the long run. The other person either isn't even aware you feel angry or upset or they don't really care that much. They are just getting on with their life so you are really only punishing yourself.

Obviously there will be big things that people 'do' to us that can cause strong emotions to arise (being told off really unfairly, a friend betraying you, etc) and we have a right to feel upset or angry. It's not about denying your emotions and it's important to feel and acknowledge them fully as they arise. Once you feel calmer though, ask yourself whether there might be something behind it that is triggering you. There nearly always is.

➤ ***I always ask myself whether The Buddha would get upset if that thing had happened to him and the answer is always 'no'!***

Learning not to react

It can be difficult to stop blaming others as it can be a really habitual way of dealing with your feelings. It's much easier to throw the emotions back at someone else than to really feel them.

Imagine someone throwing you a potato. As you catch it, it feels really hot and, because it is uncomfortable, you throw it straight back. But could you make a different choice? Perhaps you could drop the potato instead? Or you could try holding onto it and being okay with the discomfort?

Practice doing this. Next time someone says something that makes you feel angry or upset, don't throw the potato back. You can either choose to drop it (ie, not get involved in the conversation and the emotions) or you can choose to hold onto it (ie, really feel the emotions it is bringing up). You can find a sentence to help remind you – something like "This is my hot potato, not theirs".

Notice any feelings that come up when you first try this. It can be very uncomfortable but it is good to really feel these feelings. They will get easier the more you do it. Just keep practising.

➤ ***Remember that if you are kind and loving towards others then it is easier to love yourself. Try and see the best in people rather than getting angry and triggered all the time. Again, this takes practice.***

Shaming others

As well as blaming others for our feelings, something else we do is to make other people WRONG if they don't share our views and opinions.

It is particularly common on social media as people find it easier to really say what they think, often quite rudely! They think their own opinion is total truth and that everyone else is wrong. They try and convert others to their way of thinking and if that doesn't work (which it usually doesn't because who is going to respect someone who is ranting and angry?) then they put them down, calling them names or ignoring them.

➛ ***Is this you? Are you always ranting about the latest thing? Do you think anyone who doesn't agree with you is an idiot? Is your truth totally black and white and very strong and fixed?***

You might well have good intentions – perhaps you are trying to protect a minority group, or raise awareness about something you believe in passionately. But really all it does is to create a lot of anger, hatred, division and unhappiness. It is also very bad for your body as it will put you into fight and flight.

And the more you do it, the more you will get into a pattern of always looking for fault, of judging others, of seeing others as the enemy. It can create a lot of disharmony between you and other people, often affecting friendships and family relationships.

So ask yourself what is really going on. What lies behind this surface need to be angry and to be right? What is happening in your wallpaper? Here are some ideas:

- Are you being triggered by something? Perhaps you had a trauma where someone attacked you or treated you unfairly and you are still angry about that?
- Are you trying to keep yourself feeling safe by trying to control what other people think?

- Do you feel marginalised in some way by people you know or even by society?
- Do you feel as if you aren't important or can't be heard?
- Are you using your angry and strong opinions to create an identity for yourself?

Whatever you uncover about yourself, try and notice yourself ranting and stop yourself. Practice accepting others and their opinions (you might even learn something if you stop and listen). It's okay to have strong opinions but hold onto them LIGHTLY so you can be open to changing them if you hear something better.

Being open is much more powerful and intelligent than being fixed. Truth is very elusive and, as human beings, we really know very little. Our opinions are often formed from something we once read or heard or what our peer group thinks. Everything we read or hear has a bias to it depending on who wrote it or said it and why. So always start at a point of not knowing.

I totally understand that it is good to fight for things you believe in passionately and I am not trying to stop you doing that. But can you find a more positive and effective way of making changes and creating awareness? Is there something you could actually DO rather than just arguing with other people?

➛ ***What would it look like to speak out about something you are passionate about, but without any anger? People are more likely to listen to you and join you if you are giving out a positive and powerful vibration.***

Let's look at Exercise 18 to see if you are taking responsibility for your feelings, or blaming and shaming others.

EXERCISE 18 Taking responsibility

Do you often get angry or upset about the same things? Do you often experience the same strong emotion? Do you constantly get triggered by someone? Are you often angry and ranty towards others?

Sit a take some calming breaths. Now choose a situation or person that triggers you. Try and bring up some emotions by thinking about it or them. What emotions arise? Perhaps anger or hate or a sense of unfairness or frustration? Just sit with these emotions for a few moments, allowing them to fill your body without judgement.

Once you feel calmer, ask yourself what emotions lie behind these surface emotions. It's usually something like hurt or worthlessness or fear or sadness. Once you have found the feeling, sit with it and really feel it. Really own the feeling. Know that it's not really about the other person, it's about these unexpressed feelings.

Once you feel calmer, think about the person or situation you get triggered by. How do you feel about them now? If you still feel the surface emotion (ie anger) then you need to do more work.

Follow the ongoing actions below to help you take responsibility for your own feelings.

Ongoing actions

- Repeat the above exercise as often as you need to.
- Try and spot when you get triggered by other people or situations and see if you can work out what is really going on.
- Practice keeping the hot potato and feeling your emotions.
- Notice when you are being ranty and angry, and listen instead.
- See if you can find a more positive way to fight your causes.

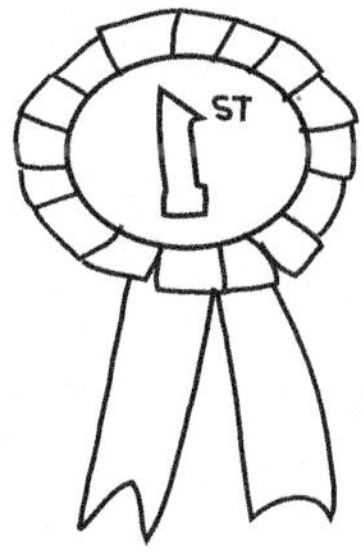

CHAPTER 3

Perfectionism

One of the biggest things that teenagers struggle with nowadays is the need to be perfect. There is a massive link between perfectionism and mental health.

➛ ***In fact, it has been shown that the higher the level of perfectionism the worse your mental health.***

Perfectionism and parenting

Perfectionism can come from how you were parented.

If you have perfectionist parents, they usually have good intentions – they just want you to be the best possible version of yourself so that you have a happy life.

Sometimes parents' own negative life experiences can act as drivers ("I didn't do anything useful with my life so I want my children to be super successful" or "I don't want my child to be bullied like I was so I need to make them really confident and popular").

We start to think that we are only loveable when we are being good or doing well. This makes us feel as if we are not loved unconditionally and it means we might reject parts of ourselves as not being acceptable.

We can also become perfectionists if our parents are very strict. When we are very young, parents are really just here to look after our physical needs and to keep us feeling safe and loved. If they start focusing too much on our behaviour and abilities then we can end up feeling unloved, unsafe and that we are never good enough. This makes us constantly strive to be perfect, either because we are scared of them or because we want them to love us.

Other causes of perfectionism

Some of us will also be perfectionists despite the fact that our parents are very laid back and loving and don't have high expectations for us.

➤ ***If this is you, why do you think this is? What is driving your perfectionism? Are you competing with a sibling? What is going on in your wallpaper? Have you decided you are no good? What untrue story are you telling yourself?***

The school system can play a part in perfectionism. When the Ofsted grading system was brought in, schools became much more results focused. Because of this there is a constant pressure from the school, teachers and even parents for you to try harder and to do better.

This means that your worth at school tends to be measured mainly by your exam results. So if you aren't doing well at these, you can often feel as if you are a failure, not just at exams but as a person. And, even if you are doing well, you are probably putting a lot of pressure on yourself to maintain your perfect grades.

Social media has also massively added to the problem of perfectionism. While home and school are all about things like ability, behaviour, confidence and success, social media is all about stuff like how you look, how popular and funny you are and how interesting your life is.

You are constantly bombarded with images of perfection from other people's posts, as well as from other forms of media. This means you constantly compare yourself with others' (often fake) happy lives.

Why is perfectionism a problem?

With all these pressures at home, at school and even during your leisure time, it's easy to decide that you are lacking in some way. You start to focus on your lack and you put pressure on yourself to do better all the time. It's like having an inner voice which is constantly criticising you.

➤ ***If you do fail at something, you don't just feel disappointed about how you did, you feel shame and anger about WHO YOU ARE. And because you don't want to feel this you try even harder to be perfect. It's a vicious circle.***

It can seem like a good thing to be a perfectionist. Think of an athlete, or a musician. It can make you work really hard and be really committed which can make you very successful. Interestingly though, perfectionism actually makes you less likely to succeed, partly because you often set yourself unreasonable goals and partly because you give up easily as you do not want to fail.

Changing your relationship with failure is key in making peace with perfectionism. Let's have a look at how we can do this.

Getting comfortable with failure

Many of us are very uncomfortable with failure. What tends to happen is that we have a bad experience with failure when we are young. Perhaps we tried to do something and failed and so we judged ourselves, or perhaps someone else said something unkind or unhelpful that made us feel bad about ourselves.

We would have experienced a strong emotion in that moment (perhaps shame or embarrassment or fear) and we would also have created limiting beliefs such as "It's not safe to fail", "I am not loveable when I fail", "I look stupid when I fail", etc. We then make a decision that it's not safe to ever fail again and so we avoid any situation where we might fail.

This means we don't try anything if there's even a tiny chance that we might fail. We stay in our comfort zone and just keep doing the things we know we CAN do. We then become very small and shut down.

➤ ***At the moment that we make the decision that we must not fail, many doors that were potentially open to us in our life will suddenly clang shut. And that's a shame.***

So here are some ideas for dealing with failure in a more positive way. I had to ask someone I know for help with writing these as I'm not good with failure. He has failed many times in his life but he just keeps pushing on as he knows failure is useful. He is now very successful and very happy.

- **Don't make it a big deal.** When we fail at something we tend to make it absolutely enormous. But remember it's just one quick moment. Don't give it so much importance.
- **Don't let it define you.** Just because you failed at that thing doesn't mean you are a failure overall as a person.
- **Don't worry about what others think.** No-one else really cares when you fail at something. Do you care if others fail? Probably not. So why is it such a big deal when you do?
- **Change the words you use.** Use positive language. Rather than saying "I failed" or "I messed it up", say things like "I need to find a different way of doing it next time" or "I'll get it eventually".
- **Learn from failure.** See failure as a thing that can teach you useful stuff about yourself and help you improve. If you fail at something, examine what you did and whether there is a better way to do it next time.
- **Set your sights on success.** When we persevere and we achieve something, it gives us a massive confidence boost. So, next time you have to do something difficult that you might fail at, remind yourself about that really positive feeling and use it to drive you forwards.

I just wanted to remind you that we are all different. If you have been trying really hard at something for a long time and just aren't getting anywhere with it then maybe it's just not your thing. Perhaps there is something better out there for you? Know when to stop. But don't do this too easily – I am not giving you a get out!

Are you a perfectionist?

Do you think you might be a perfectionist? Do you focus on results and set yourself unrealistic standards and goals? Are you very critical of yourself and have low self esteem? Do you give up easily and fear failure?

If you think you have a problem with perfectionism, ask yourself the following questions:

- In what area/s do you need to be perfect (school work, exam grades, looks, personality, behaviour, etc)?
- Where did this need for perfectionism come from (your parents, siblings, friends, school, social media, your own wallpaper, etc)?
- What are you gaining by being a perfectionist (popularity, safety, importance, feeling good about yourself)? Is it working? Are you happy?
- What are you avoiding by being a perfectionist (shame, anger, rejection, attack)? Again, is it working and are you happy?
- What might be going on in your wallpaper to trigger this perfectionism?
- How does it make you feel when you fail?
- What is the worst thing that could happen if you fail?
- What do you believe about yourself when you fail?
- What do you think others think about you when you fail?

Your answers should help you to get clearer about what is going. Notice your patterns and behaviour and try and change them. Make sure you feel any emotions that are at the root of your perfectionism – your perfectionist behaviour is probably a way of avoiding uncomfortable emotions!

Let's do Exercise 19 to get in touch with your perfectionist part.

EXERCISE 19 Your perfectionist part

Sit quietly, close your eyes and take some calming breaths. See if you can get in touch with the part of yourself that needs to be perfect.

We are now going to talk to this part of you. See if you can imagine them standing in front of you, or just get a sense of them. Let it pop up from your subconscious mind, don't overthink it.

Ask them how they are feeling. Perhaps frightened, or ashamed, or useless, or unlovable, or angry? Whatever emotion they are feeling will also come up in your body. Just sit with this feeling for a few moments. Don't resist it, just allow it without judgement.

Ask them again how they are feeling. A bit calmer perhaps? See if there is anything else they are feeling then repeat the process, really feeling all their emotions again. When they feel calmer, ask them how they would like to feel instead (calm, loved, safe, enough, etc). Just allow them to feel this, and really feel it in your own body too.

If you find this exercise difficult, don't worry. Some people will find it much harder than others. Instead, re-read the list of questions on the previous page and just sit with any emotions that come up.

Follow the ongoing actions below to help change your relationship with perfectionism and failure.

Ongoing actions

- Notice when you are being a perfectionist or avoiding failure. Is it really making you happy? Is there a better way to be?
- Try and push yourself out of your comfort zone as much as possible. Just take baby steps. Focus on the feeling of success.
- Change your relationship with failure. Remember that failure can actually be a good thing.

CHAPTER 4

The art of acceptance

In this chapter we are going to look at resistance and acceptance. We've already looked at this briefly but it's so important that I wanted to go into it in more detail.

Resistance

As human beings we easily get stuck in patterns of resisting or blocking things. We often find it easier to know what we DON'T want rather than what we DO want and so we put all our focus and energy on not wanting, of pushing away, of holding off.

When we resist something it causes problems in both our minds and our bodies. Our minds constantly fight and argue against it which is exhausting and stops us focusing on more pleasurable things. Our bodies become very tense, often going into fight or flight mode. It can make it very difficult to feel peaceful and relaxed.

➤ ***A lot of people resist life itself. They have a set idea of how they want to be, look or feel and how they want their life to be. They think they can control everything and create a perfect life for themselves. And when things don't go to plan then this makes them feel like a failure.***

We obviously do have SOME control over our lives and it's good to be focused and to have goals and plans, but there will definitely be parts of your life that you aren't in control of. I bet you didn't plan for a mental health issue?

So ask yourself what you are resisting. It might be your emotions, other people's emotions, something you don't like about yourself, another person, a situation you don't like, school, homework, food, something you have a phobia about, or even life itself? There are probably lots of little things you resist on a daily basis too (getting up, cleaning your teeth, exercise, lessons you don't like at school, homework, going to bed, etc).

Why do we resist things?

Resistance starts in the mind. Based on our beliefs and perceptions about ourselves and the world, we make a decision that something is 'wrong' or even 'dangerous'. Our body then tenses up against it and the thing feels even bigger and more undesirable (remember, what we resist gets bigger).

There are four types of things that we resist:

1. **Things we don't want to do.** This is a grumpy mind-based resistance. We don't really want to do the thing but the resistance is usually quite light and once we start doing it we feel fine (ie doing your homework or having some exercise). The resistance is often just about things like not wanting to move out of the state you are currently in, not wanting to do something because you think it will be boring or difficult, or not wanting to do something because someone else is telling you to do it.
2. **Things about your looks, abilities or personality.** This is also mind based, but can carry more weight as it can be linked to limiting beliefs or untrue stories that we have created about ourselves (ie "If I was prettier then I'd have more friends" or "If I was funnier I'd be more popular"). We can end up fighting with and resisting lots of things about ourselves that we can't change. What a waste of time and energy!
3. **Outer things.** Some people resist outer things like exams, injections, the dentist, surgery, etc. This can also include energetic and chaotic things like other people's strong emotions, noisy environments, etc. You will also feel resistance to things that you have a phobia about (ie spiders,

snakes, certain foods, germs, etc). We tense up against the outward thing that we fear so that we can try and stop ourselves from receiving it into our body as it doesn't feel safe.

4. **Our own emotions.** Another thing we resist is our own feelings and emotions. Most of us have repressed emotions and when external things come along that remind us of these feelings we tend to resist them because we don't want to feel our buried emotions.

Whatever you are resisting and whatever your reason, what you are actually trying to do is to make yourself feel safer or better by being in control. We think that if we are in control of how we look, how we act, how we feel, or of what life is bringing us then we won't have to experience things that feel unpleasant or difficult.

One of the things that many of us want to avoid feeling is chaos. We think that chaos will overwhelm us, making us feel weak and helpless. But chaos is actually life and creativity. If you block it then you are blocking parts of yourself.

So rather than tensing up against life and feeling as if it's dangerous, unpredictable, chaotic and something that you need to control, it's better to accept that life continuously unfolds and you often don't have any say over exactly how that happens. The only thing you really have any control over is how you REACT.

➤ ***Resisting things will make you closed down, negative and afraid. If you are accepting of life and open to whatever it brings you then you will feel open, curious and happy.***

So how do we start letting go of resistance?

Letting go of resistance

The best way to let go of resistance is to see what is behind it. Ask yourself the following questions to see what your resistance is about:

1. **Is it just a light grumpy mind-based resistance?** What is behind this? Perhaps you don't like other people telling you what to do? Or does it

feel boring or difficult? It may feel unpleasant to start it but you know it'll be fine once you've started. Can you find a more peaceful way of being with it?

2. **Are you resisting something about your looks, abilities or personality?** What is this showing you about yourself deep down? Why does it matter so much what you look like, what you can do and what your personality is like? Is it even all true? Does anyone else even care? Dig into your wallpaper to see what is really going on. Focus on being yourself. Find the untrue stories. Love yourself just as you are.
3. **Are you trying to protect yourself from something external?** Why do you fear this thing? Do you have limiting beliefs about how strong or capable you are? Have you got a wrong perspective on the danger of the external thing? See if you can work out where the resistance came from and why. It might have started with a trauma.
4. **Are you trying to avoid feeling some strong emotions?** What are the feelings? Where did they come from? Why are you scared of feeling them? Can you try feeling the emotions next time you are triggered? Remember that emotion is just energy and will pass quickly if you allow it. If the feeling is really big and overwhelming then take yourself somewhere quiet and just sit with it. Do the BAE technique. Use EFT if you need to reduce the intensity a bit.

Whatever your pattern is with resistance, start by noticing the things that you are resisting. This will give you valuable clues to what is going on for you. Question yourself and see where the problems are in your wallpaper.

Once you start dealing with these core things, you will start to find that you are able to live more peacefully. The external world will be more comfortable, whatever it brings. You won't need to fight against life any more and this will allow your mind and your body to relax into a state of acceptance.

Acceptance

Acceptance feels amazing. Our minds and bodies go into a state of deep relaxation and harmony. There is a lovely sense of softness and 'rightness'. For me, it's one of the best ways to feel really peaceful and content. Our minds are quiet and at rest and our bodies feel soft and safe which means they move from fight and flight mode into relaxation.

Acceptance comes from the mind. If we decide something is okay then we relax into it and become one with it. So it's all about changing the story in your mind. Why do we have a story that things should be a certain way? Why are some things right and other things wrong?

I think one problem is that when we are children we get constant messages from parents and teachers that we can have and be anything we want. Although this helps to motivate us, it's equally important to learn to accept things and to be grateful for what we actually DO have. By focusing on these things more, we will definitely feel happier.

Also, it's important to realise that you don't have any right to anything in life. Some people don't have clean water or enough food. Others only have a short life because of an illness. So stop having any judgements about what your life should and shouldn't bring you and try and accept what comes your way. You are not OWED anything by anyone.

➛ ***If something really bad DOES happen to you, it can actually have a positive side as it will bring you new learnings about yourself and life, increased emotional strength and more joy and appreciation in the long run. So next time something bad happens, rather than asking "Why is this happening to me?", try asking "What is this experience teaching me?"***

Let's do Exercise 20 to practise accepting something you have been resisting.

EXERCISE 20 Resistance to acceptance

Find the biggest thing that you are resisting – it might be a situation, an emotion, a person, something you don't want to do, something you hate about yourself, an exam you have to do, etc.

Now close your eyes and get in touch with the thing or person you are resisting. Feel the energy of that thing or person coming at you. How does it make you feel? Notice yourself tensing up against it. Where do you feel it in your body? Does it have a colour?

Now just relax your mind and body and allow the energy of the thing or person to flow into your body. Do it slowly and gradually if it feels too strong (or you can do some tapping to soften it). Let it fill your whole body and don't judge it, just keep observing until it feels less strong. If any emotions or feelings come up, really feel these too.

Now get a feeling of oneness with that thing or person, as if it's not separate from you. Let go of all your stories about it or them. Everything is part of the whole. Just sit quietly with a soft, accepting feeling in your heart.

Follow the actions below to help you become more accepting.

Ongoing actions

- Practice doing the above exercise whenever you find yourself resisting something. This will help you to become more accepting.
- Try and notice the things that you regularly resist in your life. Is there something in your wallpaper that is causing this? Perhaps there are some limiting beliefs, a phobia or a trauma?
- Are there any strong emotions that you are trying to avoid? Do some tapping on these and make sure you really feel them fully.
- Make a gratitude list and focus on all the things that you have.

SECTION 7

Going deep

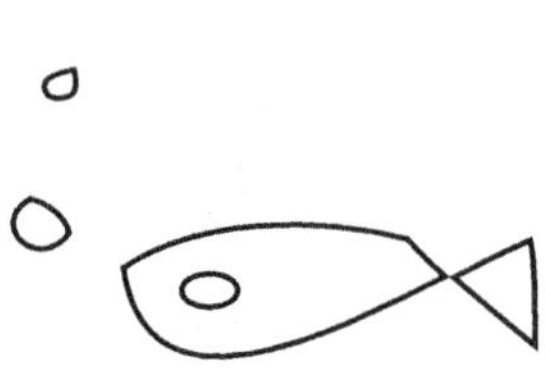

CHAPTER 1

Spirituality

In this section we are going to go a little deeper and look at some more 'out there' ideas. Let's start by looking at spirituality.

A spiritual view

It is generally accepted that as well as having a physical, mental and emotional side, we also have a spiritual side. Unless we can connect with this part of ourselves it can be difficult to feel consistently happy and safe.

Many people in the world follow a traditional religion. At the heart of religion is the concept of an all-knowing and all-powerful being who looks after us and makes us feel safe and loved (usually known as God). Religion has become less popular in this country and many people now see themselves as atheists. There has, however, been an increase in spirituality.

Spirituality is more of an inner and personal journey. Spiritual people believe in a kind of universal energy of love, which is known as 'the universe' or 'oneness' or 'love' or 'God'. We are all part of this energy and, by connecting to it, we become powerful, loving, peaceful and happy.

Spiritual people also generally believe that we are eternal and that we come here in human form to have experiences that help us to grow as souls. We return for many lifetimes and heaven is seen as a state of being that we can achieve while in human form, rather than a place we end up in.

Finding your path

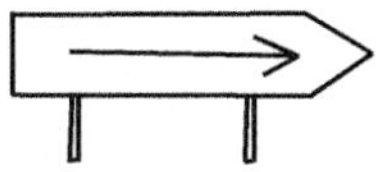

So what do you believe?

It doesn't actually really matter as long as it feels helpful for you. Perhaps you follow a religion or are more spiritual. Maybe you've never thought about it and are just getting on with your life. Or maybe you think it's all a load of rubbish and you believe that you just get one life and that's it.

There are no rights or wrongs but it might be worth asking yourself whether your beliefs are working for you.

➤ ***It's a scientifically proven fact that people who have some kind of spiritual or religious faith are generally happier than those who do not.***

If you are generally very unhappy, it might help you to reconsider your beliefs. A good starting point might be to explore spirituality. It's a massive subject and there are plenty of books and YouTube videos around. Everyone has a slightly different take on it so find something that resonates with you.

Or you could try Buddhism. This is getting increasingly popular with many celebrities. It is somewhere between a religion, a spiritual practice and a philosophy and is based around the teachings of The Buddha. Research it online if you'd like to find out more.

If you prefer something more structured and traditional, you can try joining a local church. There are lots of different types of religion to explore and they are lovely communities if you are feeling isolated or lonely.

As I've said, it doesn't really matter what you do as long as it works for you. All these practices do EXACTLY THE SAME THING – they make you feel safe, loved and connected. This puts you into a parasympathetic resting state which relaxes your mind and body, opens your heart and makes you feel happy.

➤ ***It doesn't even really matter if you don't believe 100% in it with your logical mind, just go with it and focus on the benefits!***

Connecting with your spiritual side

As I was writing this chapter, I became aware that I know quite a few people who would call themselves atheists and wouldn't be interested in spirituality. And yet they can definitely be spiritual.

Whatever your thoughts and beliefs are about religion or spirituality, it's important to realise that we DO all have a spiritual side. It's actually just about a state of being rather than anything external or anything you think or believe or follow.

Getting in touch with your spiritual side on a regular basis helps to change your perceptions about yourself and the world and will definitely help to improve your mental health.

So how do we connect to this part of ourselves?

As I already said, it's a state of being. That means that you don't really need to do anything, it's more about reconnecting to something that's always been there. Think of it like a forgotten or neglected part of yourself. All you need to do is to is to find it again and then practise living out of it.

That sounds so simple but the reality is that it takes a lot of practice. It's really worth doing though as it can make a massive difference to your thoughts and feelings, your health, your relationships and your life.

Start by building up a regular daily practice and stick to it. Remember that the subconscious mind needs a lot of repetition to make these kind of deep changes so practise as often as possible.

➤ ***Think of the house metaphor that we looked at earlier. Imagine that the house you are living in at the moment is very tatty. The walls are crumbling, the roof leaks and it's dark, cold and uncomfortable. So you are building a new house next to it, one with solid foundations, strong walls, secure doors and big windows with lovely views. It's going to be dry, warm, light and beautiful inside. But it will take a while before you have built it and can move into it. Just keep building it brick by brick.***

Below are some ideas for helping you to connect with your spiritual side. Commit to trying as many of these as possible as often as you can:

1. **Have some still time every day.** Spend some time sitting quietly every day. You can listen to some calming music or just sit and stare. 15 or 20 minutes is ideal but start with five minutes and build it up. Tune in to your body and see if you can get in touch with a sense of stillness and peace. Don't worry if it feels hard – it will get easier with practise.
2. **Connect with 'the universe'.** If you like the spiritual idea that we are connected to something bigger than ourselves, sit quietly with your eyes closed and see if you can get a sense of this. Feel it with your senses rather than trying to think it. Just be open and receptive, don't try and force anything.
3. **Connecting with nature.** For many people, one of the easiest ways to get in touch with their spiritual side is by spending time in nature. Nature contains lots of spiritual energy so if we spend time in it we can't help but start feeling it too. You probably don't like nature as you are a teenager, but try it. Let go of all your ideas about it being boring. Go for a mindful walk in your local park or the countryside. Sit outside and listen to the birds, or watch the sun rise or set. Spend time near a stream or a lake or the sea. See if you feel calmer and lighter afterwards.
4. **Being in the present moment.** It's easier to connect with our spiritual self when we are in the present moment. It helps take us out of our heads and into our bodies and our senses. Practice mindfulness to help you get into the present moment. Be aware of all your senses as this will help you to slow down and go deeper into the moment.
5. **Do things you love doing.** When we are doing something that makes us happy we naturally connect with our spiritual selves. We come out of our heads and go into our bodies and hearts. What do you love doing? What makes you feel happy? It might be music, animals, being with certain people, dancing, singing or laughing. If you can't find anything then try some new things and see what you connect with. Find your joy!

Removing blocks

If you find it really difficult to connect with your spiritual side, then what is blocking it? Remember, it is always there, so what is in the way?

Here is a list of typical blocks. I have given a few ideas for actions to take but see if you can think of your own solutions too:

- **Being too busy to find time to sit quietly**
  - Connect for five minutes when you go to bed and when you wake up
  - Plan a 15 minute session into your day in advance
  - Ask yourself what is behind your need to be so busy all the time
- **No self discipline**
  - Set some targets and use a tick chart so you can see your progress
  - Get someone else to help motivate you
  - Get an app that helps you (see the Resources section of my website)
- **Not really being present when you sit quietly**
  - Try some deep breathing to get you into your body
  - Do some exercise before you try and connect
  - Tune into your senses to calm your mind
- **Having a very busy mind which just won't turn off**
  - Ask yourself what you are thinking about and/or fearing
  - Follow a meditation to give your mind something to focus on
  - Choose times when you are tired and your mind is quieter
- **Feeling as if it's not safe to relax**
  - Listen to some beautiful music to soothe yourself
  - Tap on yourself to calm your mind and body
  - Do very short sessions and walk around when overwhelmed
- **Repressed emotions coming up when you relax**
  - Stand up and move around to help let them go
  - Spend time doing the BAE technique to really feel the emotions
  - Express the emotions physically with your voice and body
- **Thinking that you are not worth the effort**
  - Ask yourself who told you this and KNOW it is not true

  - Imagine breathing white light into your heart
  - Keep trying to connect anyway as it will help you love yourself
- **Not believing that you have a spiritual side**
  - Do the practices anyway as they will help you relax
  - Let go of any mental resistance and stories and just be open
  - Explore some other definitions of spirituality
- **Feeling as if it'll never work for you**
  - Say 'no' to these thoughts and keep connecting anyway
  - Remind yourself that it's a slow and steady practice
  - Know that you are a powerful and creative being

Forming a practice

Keep practising connecting to your spiritual side, working on any blocks. As with anything, practice makes perfect so don't give up. It probably won't feel like an amazing experience the first time you try it but as you do it more you will start to get little glimpses and over time it will strengthen.

➝ ***Many religions practice acts of devotion – for example going to church or praying. These may seem boring from the outside but what these people are doing is practising getting in touch with their spiritual side. They have learnt that it's good to build a regular practice into their life. So do the same and build a regular practice into your life.***

As you get better at it, you can start to try and connect to your spiritual side when you are caught up in stressful moments. This will help you to deal with difficult things in a much calmer way.

Let's look at Exercise 21 to help you to get in touch with your spiritual side.

EXERCISE 21 Getting spiritual

Choose a time when you feel relaxed. Sit quietly for a few moments and take some long slow deep breaths. Then close your eyes.

Now connect to your senses. Feel the sensation of your body on the chair and your clothes on your skin. Be aware of your breath flowing in and out of your nose. What can you smell? What can you taste? Half open your eyes. What forms, shapes and colours can you see?

Close your eyes again and listen to the sounds close by. Then expand your hearing out to the more distant sounds. Continue to expand it further and further out until you get a sense of stillness, peace and space beyond the sounds. Sit with this for a few moments.

Stay with this sense of peace and see if you can connect a bit deeper with it. Know that you are part of this infinite and powerful energy. Get a sense of being really perfect just as you are, of being powerful and loving. Expand all these feelings right through your body and just sit and really feel them. Everything is just perfect in this moment.

How do you feel now? Does it feel good to get in touch with this side of yourself? Remember, it's always there, you just have to connect with it. If you didn't feel much then don't worry, it can be hard to connect the first time. The more you practise it the easier it will get.

Follow the actions below to help you get more in touch.

Ongoing actions

- Practice the above exercise as often as you can.
- Practice connecting with your spiritual side. Work out what helps you to connect the most easily and do this regularly.
- Work on any blocks that might be stopping you from connecting.

CHAPTER 2

Your true self

In this chapter we are going to explore the idea that, underneath all our conditioning, we all have a perfect true self.

Reconnecting with yourself

Your true self is like the best part of you, your true nature. It exists beyond all your limited thoughts, beliefs and perceptions. It is like the childhood you – pure, untainted, true, joyful, fully present, etc.

By getting in touch with your true self again, you will feel much happier. You won't feel as if you have to do or be anything as you will know that you are perfect EXACTLY AS YOU ARE. You will have nothing to fear and you won't be able to get being you wrong.

It also won't matter what gender you are, what personality you have or what you look like. Your identity is not important, nor are your skills, your opinions or your attitudes. After all, did it matter what you could do or who you were or what you looked like when you were a small child? You were just a joyful being who was fully alive and expressing yourself.

We all have a true self and we just need to reconnect. There are cases of people suddenly rediscovering their true self and never returning to their negative state, but it's usually a long and gradual process to achieve it. And being open to the idea that you have a true self is the first step.

Losing ourselves

When we are born, we are very much our true selves. But gradually the process of being socialised, as well as traumas, means that this true self gets lost and replaced with a lot of untrue and negative stuff.

We often end up feeling as if parts of ourselves are not socially acceptable and so we feel ashamed of them. We then create a kind of false personality for ourselves so that we can hide all the negative stuff and act in a way that we think is more acceptable. We end up living out of this false personality, afraid to show too much of our real selves in case people see the bad stuff. Have a look at Box 11 for an illustration of this.

Eventually we can lose touch with who we really are and end up living in a kind of war zone between our false personality and our negative conditioning.

But at the core of this false personality and all the bad conditioning is your perfect true self. It's unchanging and will always be part of you. And it probably does show up quite a bit – perhaps when you are having a really good time with friends, or when you are doing something you really love.

So what do you think happened in your life to cover up your true self? What did your parents teach you about yourself and the world? What did your siblings, your teachers and other children at school make you believe about yourself? What did you decide about yourself based on other people's perceptions?

➛ ***What happened to make you feel like you were no longer powerful, beautiful, perfect and unique?***

Unfortunately, nearly all of us have lost touch with our true selves these days. Most of us are judgmental, self limiting and fearful. I'm not sure why this has happened but it is probably to do with the way our society is structured. I'm sure the media plays its part too as it constantly tells us how to be and how to look and is generally VERY judgmental.

BOX 11 How your true self gets covered up

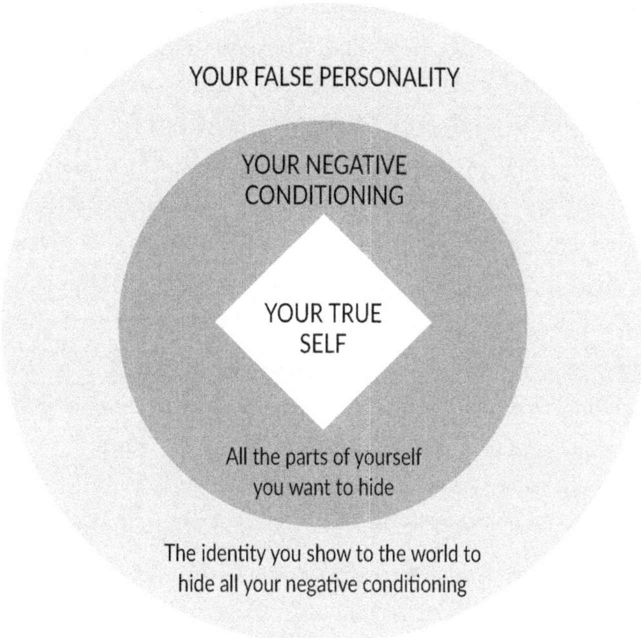

All of this means that you will get socialised to be judgmental, self limiting and fearful too. Even if your parents don't teach you this way of being, you will probably pick it up from school and from the media and society.

It's unlikely that there will have been anyone in your life to help you to stay connected with your true self. You, along with most of your generation, will have to find your own way back.

Reconnecting with your true self

It's a journey to get back in touch with your true self. Here are a few ideas:

1. **Keep connecting to your spiritual side.** When you are in touch with your spiritual side it is easier to get a sense of who you REALLY are. Sit and ask "Who am I really, underneath all my conditioning?". Don't force any answers, just allow things to come up.
2. **Reconnect with your childhood self.** Find a memory of when you felt really good. Spend some time with this younger you. Make them bigger and more colourful in your mind so you can really connect. When something difficult happens, see how they would react. Get in touch with them regularly as this will help remind you of who you REALLY are.
3. **Follow your joy.** Another way to get more in touch with your true self is to do things that make you happy. What do you love doing? What makes you feel alive? Who do you like to hang out with? Listen to your gut feelings, your emotions and your instincts as these will help guide you back to who you really are and what feels right for you.

It's often quite hard to get a sense of your true self and, as with everything, practice is key. I've also noticed that even if you do manage to connect with your true self, it's very easy to lose the connection again. This usually happens whenever we are busy. And stuff like stress, negative thoughts, fear and other strong negative emotions will definitely disconnect us.

So start to get in touch with your true self regularly throughout the day. Notice the things that make it easier to connect. And notice the things that take you away from your true self. Spend time really being you.

I'm not saying you have to live out of this space all the time. You are a teenager and you won't be wanting to sit around doing peaceful things all the time, that's boring. However, it's good to balance out your other activities with some of these more restful ones, especially if you struggle with your mental health.

Now complete Exercise 22 to practise getting in touch with your true self.

EXERCISE 22 Connecting with your true self

Close your eyes and let your attention drop down into your body, like sand through an egg timer. Take a few calming deep breaths.

Now, staying very open, see if you can get in touch with how you felt as a really young child. Pick a time when you felt really happy. Perhaps you have a memory you can think of? Get a sense of how it felt to be truly you, not to filter anything out or hide anything or have to worry about what anyone else was thinking about you. See yourself expressing yourself and feeling happy. Let this feeling of really being you fill your body right now.

Can you see that you were perfect just as you were, and that you still are? Do you need to hang onto these untrue thoughts, feelings and beliefs that you created to keep you feeling safe? This true self part of you still exists inside you and you can reclaim it whenever you want. You may have forgotten it but it hasn't forgotten you.

Practice getting in touch with this younger true self energy regularly. It will get easier the more you do it. Do it before you go to sleep and when you wake up. You can also connect every time you get a quiet moment during the day. The more you do it the stronger it will get and the less your problems will seem to matter.

Follow the actions below to help you get in touch with your true self.

Ongoing actions

- Do the above exercise as often as possible.
- Find other ways to get in touch with your true self (see the list of suggestions earlier in this chapter) and practise them every day.
- Work on your wallpaper to help you let go of your negative conditioning and false personality so your true self can show up.

CHAPTER 3

It's all an illusion

In the last chapter we explored the idea that we all have a true self that we have lost touch with because of our childhood conditioning.

Now we are going to look at how we spend most of the time living out of a complete illusion and how being our true self can help to free us from this so that we can feel happy again.

Your 3D web

We have looked at the idea that we have a background wallpaper to all our thoughts, feelings and perceptions. This wallpaper contains all our untrue stories and limiting beliefs, our judgements about ourselves and our traumatic life experiences.

We live out of this wallpaper and it defines our reality. But is it really true?

I want you to imagine your wallpaper in 3D, like a web. This web contains all the things that are in your wallpaper – your thoughts, perceptions, beliefs, feelings and emotions. The web might be beautiful and soft and silvery or it might be black and sticky and messy and tangled.

➤ ***Based on what your wallpaper contains, how do you think your web might look?***

Now imagine that stuck right in the middle of this 3D web is you. You are completely surrounded by your web, entangled in it. You are living from it and your whole personality and all your actions are totally defined by it.

See if you can get a sense of standing back and looking at your web and yourself stuck in it. Do you really want to be in there? Is it making you happy? Who were you before you created this web and got stuck in it? Who would you be without this web?

➛ ***Understand that you are NOT this web. You are NOT these thoughts, feelings and beliefs. You are SO MUCH MORE than this.***

Building your web

As I said in the last chapter, you were probably being your true self when you were a very young child. You would have been happy and carefree, accepting yourself totally, expressing your emotions freely, not worried about what other people were thinking and not needing to be or look a certain way. Your wallpaper would have been really beautiful.

But as you gradually became conditioned by your environment, experiences and the people around you, you would have changed your behaviour, thoughts and beliefs in order to feel safe, worthy, 'normal', loved and acceptable. Your wallpaper would have started to change, becoming a dense, dark and tangled web.

And as you spent more time at school and with your peer group, this process would have continued. By the time you became a teenager, you would have been stuck in a big and complicated web of limiting beliefs and negative behaviours.

If you are lucky your web won't be too bad. Perhaps your childhood was pretty good and you had plenty of love and were accepted for who you are. Your web will be less dense, lighter and easier to get out of. But perhaps you had a really miserable childhood and you felt unloved and misunderstood and you've been beating yourself up ever since? Your web will be more entangled and dense and dark.

➤ ***I generally find that if you are intelligent, sensitive and creative then your web will be more tangled. This is because you are more reactive and complex and your brain forms very creative and clever loops and connections.***

As we get older it gets harder to detach from our web. We become more and more defined by it and it becomes more habitual and programmed in. So now is a really good time for you to become aware of it and to start the journey of detaching from it.

Detaching from your web

There are two ways of detaching from your web:

1. Unpick it by working on and clearing all the thoughts, perceptions, traumas and negative beliefs that are in your wallpaper. This will naturally take you back towards your true self.
2. Focus on getting back in touch with your true self. The more you do this the less you will find yourself identifying with all the stuff in your web.

The best way forwards is to do both these things. It's hard to get in touch with your true self when you are so triggered by your web. And it's hard to clear your web when you are not in touch with your true self.

Again, it's important to see the above process as a journey rather than something that needs to be FIXED or GOT RID OF. In the process of this journey you will learn many things about yourself and you will become a stronger, better and wiser person. Don't give yourself any timescales, just make a commitment to make a first step.

Let's look at each of these ways of detaching from your web in more detail.

1. Unpicking your web

To unpick your web, the first useful thing to do is to try and define roughly what's in your wallpaper. Look at the first section to refresh your memory. What story have you created about yourself? Are you being yourself or trying to be like everyone else? How much do you love yourself? Have you had any traumas? How have all these things defined you? What beliefs have you formed? What don't you want to feel/experience/be/accept about yourself or the world deep down?

If you are creative, you can try and draw your web. If you don't like drawing, you could write each thing on a separate post-it note and stick them all on a big piece of paper, perhaps drawing lines to link them all together. Find a way that works for you. And do keep adding things as there will be a lot of stuff in your web that you are not aware of and more stuff will be revealed to you the more you unpick it.

Once you have a better understanding of your web, you can start to clear it. We will be creating a personalised action plan later in the book which will help you with this.

2. Getting back in touch with your true self

We looked at some ways to get in touch with your true self in the previous chapter, including connecting to childhood memories of when you felt happy and free, and also regularly connecting with your spiritual side. Doing things that make you feel happy will also guide you back towards your true self.

Another idea is to practise visualising your web with yourself stuck in it. By standing back from yourself and your web, it will remind you that it's not you and that you are more than this. Try and do this every day. And do it when you feel really stuck in your thoughts or are feeling anxious and negative. This will help you start to detach.

You can use positive affirmations as you visualise your stuck self: "I am not this", "I am so much more than this", "I choose to let this web go", etc. The universal affirmations are also helpful for getting back in touch with your true self ("I am power", "I am beauty", "I am love", "I am peace").

Don't worry if it feels really difficult and daunting to free yourself from your web and connect with your true self at this stage. Hopefully it's helpful to have this new perspective on your problems and might give you a feeling of hope and start loosening up all those fixed ways of thinking.

Community and society webs

As well as our own 3D webs, we are also trapped in the larger webs of the community we live in and our country. These webs tell us how to think, how to be and what to do. They influence our personalities and behaviour more than we realise.

It's difficult to free ourselves from these larger webs as there is a kind of CODE OF CONDUCT for how to be within each community and country. At the moment you won't have much control over who you live with and which community or country you are part of so all you can do is to make sure you are true to yourself as much as possible.

You will need to keep this in balance though because we are social beings and it's important to fit in so that we have the support and connection of a community. If you go against it too much, you will end up being an outcast which won't make you happy either.

As you get older, you will have more choice about the community you live in. You can create the right community for yourself through your choice of partners, friends, work, hobbies and interests. And if you don't like the country you live in, you can even move to another one!

Complete Exercise 23 to have a look at your 3D web in more detail.

EXERCISE 23 Exploring your 3D web

Sit quietly, close your eyes and take a few calming breaths.

Get a sense of your wallpaper as a 3D web, full of all your thoughts, feelings, perceptions and beliefs. Now imagine standing back and seeing yourself stuck in the middle of this web, trapped in all the stuff you have created to protect yourself.

Can you see that there's a part of you that is looking at yourself stuck in your web? This is your true self. Just allow yourself to connect with this part of you for a few minutes. How does it feel?

See if you can get a sense of peace, stillness and expansiveness as you watch yourself in your web. Send love and acceptance towards this stuck part of you.

If you find this exercise difficult then don't worry. It's worth practising it as the more you do it the easier it will become. It's important to try and get in touch with your true self as it will help you to realise that you are so much more than your thoughts, beliefs and perceptions.

Follow the actions below to help you detach from your web.

Ongoing actions

- Practice the above exercise to remind yourself that you are so much more than your web.
- Write a list of all the things that are in your wallpaper. Or you can draw it or find another creative way to express it.
- Keep working on all the stuff in your wallpaper as this will help you to detach from your web.

CHAPTER 4

Human Design

In this final chapter we are going to look at something which, to me, shows that we are all designed to be different. This can really help you to understand and be yourself.

Human Design

I came across Human Design a few years ago. It's a system which defines your personality based on which planets are in alignment when you were born.

Now, being quite a scientifically-minded person, I have never really believed in these kind of things. How can our personalities be influenced by the position of the planets? It all sounds a bit WOO-WOO and strange.

But, being very open minded and having a lot of respect for the (highly intelligent and logical) person who introduced me to this, I let them read my Human Design chart. I was totally blown away by it. It just made total sense of me in a way that nothing ever had before.

I was instantly able to drop some of my ideas about myself – of not being enough, of being boring, weak, weird and too sensitive. I saw myself in a new light and a new me started to emerge. Human Design has made a massive difference to how I feel about myself, as well as to my relationships, my work and how I parented my daughter.

I went on to do readings for friends and family and, every time, it was so accurate and insightful. So I have accepted that although we don't yet understand the science behind Human Design it's very valid and useful.

In Box 12 there are two Human Design charts. The one on the left is mine and the one on the right is Angelina Jolie's (no significance, just a random celebrity!).

These charts are made up of centres (the squares, diamonds and triangles) and channels (the connecting lines which run between the centres). You can see that some of these centres and channels are filled in and some are white. If the whole chart was fully coloured in then that would represent the whole of the human race. We are all part of this whole and we each get different bits of it. As you can see from the two charts, my filled in bits are different to Angelina's filled in bits, meaning that we are both different.

How it can help us

Human Design charts show many things about us, including how emotional we are, how we think, where our strengths and gifts lie, how we make decisions, our purpose, and the things that we struggle with and

BOX 12 Human Design charts

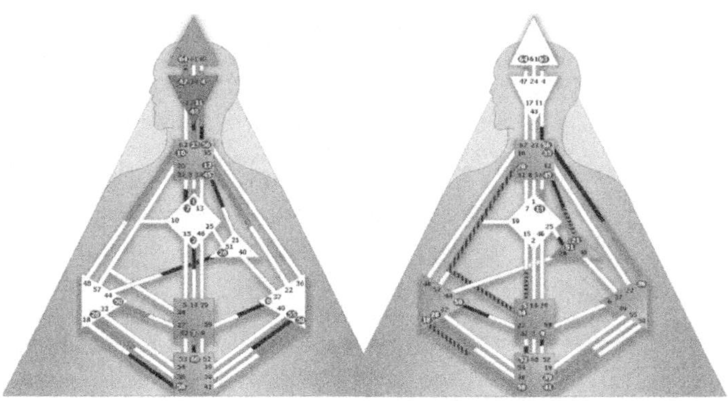

Me Angelina Jolie

why. I am not going to go into detail about how it all works as it's quite complicated. I am only really using it to show you that we ARE all different.

When I found this system it provided me with the evidence that we are all different and that we are all part of a whole. It was such a relief to me that I didn't have to conform to this GENERIC person that society expected me to be and that I could just be my unique self instead.

Understanding yourself at this level is so useful and it really helps you to have a more fulfilling and happier life. I really wish I'd seen my chart when I was your age. It would have helped me with so many things.

Having said that, we do have a natural built in way of knowing what we enjoy and what we are good at and which people are good for us, so we don't have to see our charts to know ourselves. Our emotions and our gut feelings and instincts are there to guide us and if we learn to listen to these and act on them then we will definitely become more ourselves.

➤ ***I am living my design right now by writing this book – my chart shows that my strengths are to take abstract and complicated ideas and structure them in a simple way so that I can communicate them clearly to other people in order to help them to change!***

If you want to know more about Human Design, have a look on the internet. There are plenty of sites that let you create a free chart and you can then read up about what it means. Or get the book *Human Design* by Chetan Parkyn. This gives you a detailed explanation of your chart in a clear and easy to read format. Or you can get a professional Human Design reading – there are plenty of people who offer this on the internet.

You might find Human Design a bit too much to take in and feel as if it's not really your thing. We are all different and some of you will have more logical minds rather than open abstract minds. It means you will be more closed to things that are a bit 'out there' and you will like hard and scientifically proven facts. This is great as it stops the really 'out there' people getting too 'out there' so it's healthy for society. Hopefully you can still acknowledge that we are all different though?

SECTION 8

Exploring mental health issues

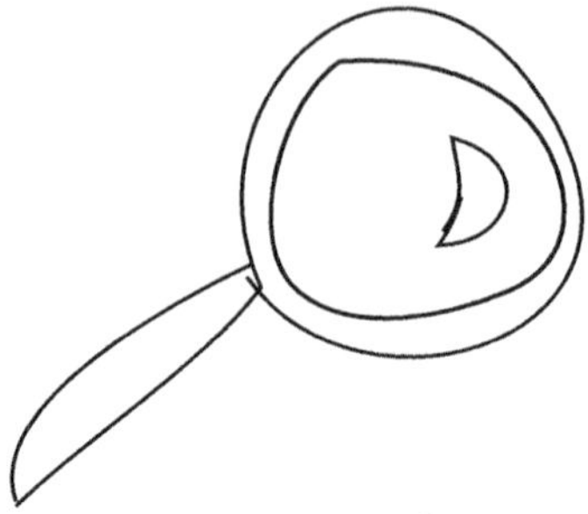

CHAPTER 1

Using symptoms as clues

We have looked at a lot of stuff so far in this book and hopefully you are beginning to have some realisations and learnings about yourself. Are you starting to see your mental health in a whole new light?

As I said at the beginning of this book, mental health issues are not random things that just HAPPEN to you. They are symptoms of your negative thoughts, limiting beliefs, skewed perceptions and mishandled emotions.

➛ ***In other words, most people are creating their own mental health symptoms at a deep subconscious level.***

The only way to get rid of your mental health symptoms FOR GOOD is to get in touch with who you really are, to love and accept yourself at a deep level and to let go of your traumas, limiting beliefs and untrue stories. Your thoughts will then start to change and your mental health will improve.

I just wanted to repeat what I said in the introduction, that there may well be chemical and physical reasons for some mental health issues. Having said that, I believe that our bodies are very much governed by our minds and that if we are happy, relaxed and flowing then our bodies will rebalance themselves.

So for now I'd suggest that you put aside any thoughts that your mental health issue may be being caused by something chemical or physical and focus on making some deeper changes to yourself. I guarantee that this will have a big impact on your mental health.

For some people, knowing that you are creating your symptoms might feel like a relief. I know it did for me. It gives you some power over the situation and also a sense of hope that you can change it and that you are not a helpless victim.

For others it can feel like another burden and an opportunity to beat yourself up ("Why am I so useless/I'm so messed up/other people don't do this so why do I?").

➤ ***If you feel like this, it's important to make peace with it otherwise it's just another big negative dollop to add to your wallpaper.***

Be kind to yourself, it's okay. People who suffer from mental health issues are usually sensitive, creative and intelligent. It comes with the territory. Have compassion for yourself. You are not alone – these kind of problems are very common and you are one step ahead of everyone else as you are reading this book and doing something about it!

What are your symptoms showing you?

Whatever mental health issues you are struggling with, it's good to look at your specific mental health 'symptoms' as they can give you valuable clues about what is going on for you. This in turn will help you uncover where your thinking and beliefs might be defective.

So in this section we are going to look at each mental health issue in turn and I will make some suggestions for what sort of things could be at the root of each issue. These are only my suggestions and, as it will vary from person to person, you might need to dig further to work out exactly what is going on for YOU.

Please read this whole section rather than just skipping to your relevant issue. Remember, your issue is a symptom rather than something you have randomly 'got' so you will almost certainly have other 'symptoms' and this will give you more clues about what is going on for you. For example,

BOX 13 Tapping to loosen things up

1. **Tap on the issue in a global way**

   Start by tapping on your problem in a general or global way. It's a useful way of loosening it up. Try something like:

   - "Even though I feel... (ie, anxious, depressed, etc), I'm okay".
   - "Even though I have... (ie, OCD, an eating disorder, etc), I'm okay".
   - "Even though I have this horrible mental health issue, I'm okay".

2. **Tap on how having the issue makes you feel**

   Then tap on how your issue makes you feel. How you feel about it can create more problems than the actual issue itself.

   - "Even though my... (ie anxiety/phobia etc) makes me feel..., I'm okay".
   - "Even though my mental health issue is ruining my life and that makes me feel..., I'm okay".
   - "Even though I'm feeling completely overwhelmed and don't know where to start with my mental health issue, I'm okay".

3. **Tap to acknowledge that you are creating your issue**

   Do a round to acknowledge that you are creating your own mental health issue and how that makes you feel:

   - "Even though it is possible that I am creating my own mental health issue and that makes me feel..., I'm okay".

4. **Tap to get yourself unhooked from really stuck feelings and beliefs**

   Some mental health disorders can be very challenging. Your feelings and beliefs about yourself will feel SO true that you may not be able to see any other way of looking at things. Acknowledge this by saying something like:

   - "Even though it feels REALLY difficult to change this issue, I'm okay".

- "Even though I really truly believe that I am... (ie overweight/ugly/defective/stupid/stuck/no good etc), I'm okay".
- "Even though my beliefs about myself feel really fixed and true and I will NEVER be able to change them, I'm okay".
- "Even though I absolutely CAN'T love or accept myself and never will be able to, I'm okay".
- "Even though everything feels so enormous and difficult to change and I feel as if there's no point trying, I'm okay"

5. **Tap to feel more positive**

You can also create some positive statements to help you shift deeply held feelings of stuckness. Make sure you clear your negative feelings down a bit first though or your mind won't accept them:

- "Even though it feels very difficult to change my mental health issue, I am open to the possibility that I CAN do this".
- "Even though I totally believe that I will always feel like this, I am open to a miracle happening".
- "Even though this all feels very difficult, there's a small part of me that knows EXACTLY how to let go of my issue and to feel really happy again".
- "Even though I feel small, weak and helpless, I am open to knowing that I am connected to something much bigger and more powerful than me and that I can use this strength to help me".
- "Even though part of me feels so overwhelmed and hopeless, I know that my true self can handle all of this just fine".
- "Even though I feel so alone and scared, I am a beautiful being and it's time to shine my light in the world".

someone with an eating disorder might well also suffer from anxiety, overwhelm, negative thoughts and lack of confidence.

Before you start working on your issue, it can also be helpful to do some tapping on how your issue actually makes you feel. This will help to loosen it all up a bit. Follow the tapping suggestions in Box 13 on the previous two pages.

CHAPTER 2

Common mental health disorders

In this chapter we are going to focus on the more common and well known mental health issues.

Some of them have proper official sounding names but don't get too caught up in these labels. They are still just a bunch of symptoms that someone has given a fancy name to and it's important not to let them DEFINE YOU. Remember, you are SO much more than these symptoms so don't buy into them too much.

So let's look at each mental health issue in turn to see what it might be showing you about yourself and your wallpaper. Read each section and use the questions in Box 14 on the next page to help you dig into your issue.

And remember to do some tapping on how your mental health issue makes you feel too as this will help you let go of it (see Box 13).

➤ ***Please note that I am not an expert on the more complex mental health issues in this chapter and I won't be going into a lot of detail about them. If you have a big and complicated issue that has really taken over your life then do seek appropriate help from a professional.***

BOX 14 Digging into your issue

The following is a list of useful questions you can ask yourself when you are trying to get to the bottom of your mental health issue. Write down your answers and see if they give you any clues:

- When did it start?
- What was going on in your life at that time or before it?
- Did you experience a trauma that might have created your issue?
- What is the very worst thing about this issue for you?
- What is your very worst fear when you think of this issue?
- What are you trying to avoid by having this issue?
- What emotions are you frightened of feeling?
- What are you trying to achieve or get by having this issue?
- What do you have to believe about yourself to have this issue?
- What other beliefs might be contributing to the issue?
- What qualities do you think you lack that, if you had, would help you overcome your issue?
- Does this issue give you anything positive that you'd find it hard to let go of?
- If you could change anything in your life, what would it be?
- What is going on in your wallpaper that might be contributing to this issue:
  - Are you being yourself or are you constantly comparing yourself with others?
  - Have you made up any untrue stories about yourself?
  - Do you love (or even like) yourself?

Your answers should help you to get more clarity about what is really going on for you and what you need to work on and change.

Stress

Stress is a general term for stuff like anxiety, overwhelm, phobias, negative thinking, worry, obsessions, etc.

If you are someone who always feels stressed, the first thing to do is to work out exactly what you mean by 'stress' and what might be causing it.

So what does stress mean for you? Are you stressed because you constantly have anxious thoughts? Do you feel unloveable, unconfident, powerless or unsafe? Do you have a phobia or an unresolved trauma? Do you have issues with your looks or your abilities? Are there certain situations that make you really stressed? Do you get more stressed around other people? Is there someone in particular that makes you feel stressed?

Make a list of all the answers you came up with. You can also ask yourself the questions in Box 14.

Once you have defined your stress, you will need to dig deep and see what is really behind it. What is going on in your wallpaper? Try and find the defective thinking or the untrue story you have created. Or there might be a trauma that you need to look at.

Anxiety

Anxiety is actually fear. It is like a low-level nagging feeling and is caused by constant negative thoughts. It is very common and many teen (and adult) issues have anxiety at their core.

Anxiety mainly comes from not feeling as if we are enough. If we don't feel strong enough, capable enough, good enough, loveable enough, etc, then it will feel as if life is coming at us and that we won't be able to deal with it. We may worry that we will fail, not cope, lose control, not meet others' expectations or that we'll be rejected or get ill or even die.

Here are some common thoughts which might be creating anxiety:

- I'm not enough (I'm not clever/loveable/powerful/good enough).
- I'm too much (too loud, too chaotic, too weird, too different, too big).

- I'm overwhelmed (everything is too much, too difficult, too loud).
- I'm not safe (I am vulnerable, life is dangerous, something will get me).
- I'm frightened of... (illness, dying, other people, germs, failure).
- Something is going to go wrong (failing, not coping, rejection, accidents, disasters, illness, dying).

There will also be specific things that might have come from an unresolved trauma, for example fear of going in cars if you've been in a road accident

What do you worry about? Can you see if you can work out where you don't feel as if you are enough? What's your deepest fear about yourself? Is it actually true? Who did you learn it from? What limiting beliefs are behind it? Have a good look at your wallpaper for clues. Try and find the defective thinking or the untrue story you have created. Or perhaps there is a trauma? Use the questions from Box 14 to help you.

➛ ***If you can't get to the bottom of what is making you anxious, every time you feel anxious see what is going on in that moment. What are you thinking or feeling about yourself or others? Where are you not enough? Are you being reminded of a past trauma? Are you projecting into the future and imagining something bad?***

Panic attacks

A panic attack is a feeling of intense fear and includes symptoms like palpitations, a racing heart, sweating, trembling and shortness of breath. People often think they are having a heart attack and are going to die.

A panic attack is basically a big fight or flight response. The body is flooded with stress hormones which cause symptoms like a racing heart and shallow breathing. You will then start wondering "Why is my heart going crazy?" and "Why can't I breathe?". This creates even more fear and more stress hormones are released. And so it's a vicious circle of panic and hormones which create more symptoms and more panic.

Panic attacks are usually caused by ongoing stressful and overwhelming situations. You will have been repressing a lot of strong emotions and the body just can't hold it all in any longer and needs to express it.

You can also get panic attacks when you are relaxing. This is because the body is releasing all the repressed stress and overwhelm. Remember, the freeze response is released when we relax.

Whatever pattern your panic attacks take, ask yourself what fear patterns are behind them. What makes you feel overwhelmed? What can't you cope with? Do you have a phobia about something that makes you panic, or is there an unresolved trauma that is triggering you? And how are you dealing with your emotions? Ask yourself the questions in Box 14 too.

One of the problems with panic attacks is that once you have had one you are scared that you'll have another one. It's good to do some tapping on this fear. Work on yourself when you are not actually having a panic attack and see if you can get in touch with the feeling of panic. Clear it down by tapping on the feelings in your body and use the BAE technique to really feel any strong emotions. This should help to calm your panic attacks a bit until you have had time to address the underlying cause.

And if you do have a panic attack, just remember that it's NOT going to kill you. Try and go with it. Be aware that the more you panic the stronger it will get. Burn up some of the stress hormones by moving about and expressing the energy in your body. Cry, shout, kick, jump up and down, run on the spot, hit something. Be like a little child. Let your body act out what it needs to do and just go with it! Remember it's trying to help you.

Phobias

Phobias are an irrational fear of something specific. You will try and avoid that thing as much as possible but, if you are in a situation where you cannot avoid it, you can become extremely overwhelmed and fearful.

Phobias often form as the result of a trauma. During the trauma we may have experienced feelings that were so unpleasant that we never want to feel them again. This makes us avoid any situation that could bring up these emotions.

➛ ***When I was about 16, I was chased by a boy holding a spider. It was so terrifying that I became hysterical. Every time I saw a spider after that I would freak out, especially if there were other people around who I thought might chase me with the spider. One day my daughter had a massive spider in her room. There was no one else to help so I had to catch it. I can still remember that feeling of overwhelming terror as I lowered the pint glass over it and slid a postcard underneath. All that fear came right up but I stayed with it because I had to and I put that spider out in the garden. And now I'm much less scared of spiders!***

If you have a phobia, see if there's a trauma behind it and do some clearing on it. Also ask yourself which emotions you are trying to avoid. Then let yourself feel them. Do it slowly and gently using the BAE technique.

Phobias can also represent something big in your wallpaper. I had a client who was scared of flying. His fear was specifically around sudden mechanical failure of the aeroplane. From this, we found that he had a fear of his body failing. And that led to stuff about not feeling safe, not feeling powerful, not trusting his body. So phobias can be very useful signposts.

Use the questions in Box 14 to help you to dig into what is really going on with your phobia.

Obsessive Compulsive Disorder (OCD)

People with OCD usually have obsessive thoughts and urges and this drives them to carry out some kind of behaviour which helps to soothe and get rid of the obsession.

Common obsessions might include fear of contamination (from germs, bodily fluids, chemicals), fear of losing control, fear of being overwhelmed and fear of not being perfect. Common behaviours might include washing and cleaning, checking, and rituals around words or numbers.

OCD can be complicated but at the root of it will lie things like excessive anxiety, specific and overwhelming fears, a trauma that hasn't been dealt with, resistance, self hatred, self rejection, etc.

If you have OCD, what is going on for you? What are you trying to avoid or to gain from your behaviour? What don't you want to feel? What triggers it? How do you feel about yourself? What are you REALLY frightened of and why? Stand back from it and try and get some clarity.

As with phobias, there is often a trauma behind OCD. Ask yourself what was happening in your life just before the OCD started. Are you trying to avoid feeling something, perhaps an emotion? What did the trauma make you believe about yourself and life?

Use the questions in Box 14 to see if you can find out more. Dig deep and look for your dysfunctional thinking. The OCD could be a manifestation of something that is skewed in your wallpaper.

Depression

It's very common to feel a bit down sometimes but depression is more overwhelming and persistent. It can be hard to lift your mood even when you are doing something you really enjoy.

There are a few things that can lead to depression:

- **Hopelessness.** When we feel really hopeless about ourselves or a situation or our lives in general, we can end up getting depressed. It feels as if there is no point to anything. What are you feeling hopeless about? Or do you feel hopeless about YOURSELF and, if so, why?
- **Life is difficult.** Some people find it really hard to cope with difficult things. They just don't have good coping strategies. This can lead to depression if a lot of difficult things happen. Has your life been difficult? Why do you think you find it hard to cope with difficulty?
- **Repressed emotions.** Depression can be caused by repressed emotions. If we don't allow our emotions to flow, this can make us feel very blocked and shut down. Are you repressing your emotions? Why?

- **Trauma.** Some people get depressed after a big trauma. It's the body's way of shutting you down a bit while you process and heal the trauma. Have you shut down because of a trauma?
- **Protection.** It has been suggested that depression is the body's way of shutting down to keep you safe. If you perceive life to be really stressful and dangerous it makes sense to shut down and hide away to stay safe. Are you so stressed that you are subconsciously shutting down?
- **Grief.** When we lose someone we love, grief is a natural process. Some people can end up getting stuck in their grief and spiralling down into depression. Are you struggling to cope with losing someone?
- **Other mental health problems.** If you have a big mental health problem you can end up getting depressed. These issues have a big impact on your life, especially if you can't find a way out of them. Is this what is happening to you?
- **Genetics.** Depression does often run in families. As I've said before, it's as much to do with how your family thinks and deals with problems. It can also be learned and copied behaviour. Do one of your parents suffer from depression? How similar are your ways of dealing with the world?
- **Physical causes.** Depression can certainly be made worse by things like hormonal imbalances, nutritional deficiencies, diet, lack of exercise, lack of sunlight, posture etc. We will look in more detail at these in Section 9. Ask yourself what your diet is like. Do you look after your body?

Once you have explored what might be causing your depression on a superficial level, dig down and see if you can work out what is behind your reactions. Why are you feeling hopeless or overwhelmed? What are you thinking or believing that means you can't cope when other people can?

Use the questions in Box 14 to help you explore your depression. Keep looking at your background wallpaper for clues. What are you thinking, feeling or doing that might be creating these beliefs and perceptions?

➤ ***When you are depressed, it is common to have other symptoms like anxiety, negative thinking, lack of confidence, eating disorders, etc. These can give you a clue about what might be behind your depression.***

Nervous breakdowns

Nervous breakdowns are like a big mental crisis. You will experience intense mental distress and will often be unable to function properly.

They can occur when we have been stuck in a lot of negative and dysfunctional thinking, repressing our emotions and feelings and resisting lots of things in our life. They can also happen when we have experienced overwhelming traumas that we can't process.

➤ ***Sometimes they happen AFTER the trauma or event, when we have relaxed. It's like our minds are saying "Now that's all over I can let go and release all the energy of the stress and the emotions". This often plunges us back into negativity and keeps us stuck in a bad pattern.***

So why do we have these breakdowns? Basically our system just gets overwhelmed and cannot function any longer in that way. There is a breakdown (which can be sudden or gradual) so that we are forced to stop what we are doing and change our ways.

Unfortunately, nervous breakdowns are seen as something very negative in our society, as if we have 'lost the plot' or gone mad. So when we have them we tend to fear and resist them which just adds even more into the pot. We also beat ourselves up as being defective in some way.

If you can see these breakdowns as your mind being very intelligent and trying to help you then they can be useful in the long run. It's like your mind saying "Stop! I can't do this any more! I need a complete break and you need to make some serious changes to your thinking and your life!"

You will need to examine every aspect of what you are thinking, feeling and believing, how you are handling emotions, what traumas are affecting you, etc. Ask yourself the questions in Box 14. Dig deep into your wallpaper as there will definitely be something big going on.

It's probably best to get some help and support as you may not have the energy or drive to do this level of work when you are in such a bad place. But make sure that you fully commit to making some big changes.

Hearing voices

Hearing voices and sounds in your head can be very scary. But it is actually more common than you might think, with one in ten people experiencing it at some point. It is usually a symptom of poor mental health and is associated with stress, anxiety, depression and trauma.

➤ ***Hearing voices is different to intrusive thoughts. It sounds like someone else's voice speaking, not yours. Sounds can include voices talking to or about you, music, animal noises or background noises.***

For some people the voices can be positive, helping them to manage their emotions or to make decisions. For others it can be more negative with the voices being threatening or unkind.

No one seems to know what causes these voices but what is clear is that they get worse when we are more stressed. There's a clue here! I would suggest that when you are having a lot of strong and obsessive thoughts that in the end the mind needs to let the energy out (a bit like when we repress too much emotion).

If YOU hear voices, start to notice what triggers them. You can also learn to react differently. Remember, these voices are just part of you, they can't hurt you. Perhaps they just need to be heard? Blocking and repressing them will make them stronger so try and make friends with them. You might need to do some tapping or get some other help to do this.

Really what these voices are showing you is that you need to make some changes to your mental health. Answer the questions in Box 14 and look at your wallpaper to see what is really going on. Are you are being really hard on yourself? Or perhaps there is a trauma that has triggered it?

Suicidal thoughts

If you sometimes get suicidal thoughts, start by saying right now "Even though my life sometimes feels so terrible that I don't want to be me any more, I accept myself and all my thoughts and feelings". It's very powerful even just to acknowledge this out loud.

People usually feel suicidal because they just can't see another way out. Know right now that there is ALWAYS another way out and, just because you can't see it right now, it doesn't mean it doesn't exist. Just by having the right conversation with someone, or some useful therapy sessions, or reading a helpful book, you can begin to feel differently.

Some people use suicide as a cry for help. Although unsuccessful suicide attempts CAN help get the right help and attention, it's devastating for the people that love us and is also very dangerous. It's far better to talk to someone about how you are feeling so that you can get the right help.

So, if you ever suffer from suicidal thoughts, ask yourself why. Is it because you feel hopeless about yourself? Or perhaps you feel overwhelmed by a big mental health issue? Ask yourself the questions in Box 14. Dig down and find out what is going on in your wallpaper. See if you can find the defective thinking that might be creating the suicidal feelings.

➤ ***Although it all feels massive and real to you right now and there doesn't appear to be a way out, you have just got yourself stuck in some bad thought patterns. I promise you 100% that you WILL feel happy again.***

If you are feeling really bad, you will probably be thinking that you are not worth the effort. But you are – you are a beautiful perfect soul, just a bit lost at the moment. Things can change really quickly with EFT so please don't give up on yourself. Start tapping today.

And please tell an appropriate adult as soon as possible. If you don't have anyone to turn to, see the list of support organisations in the Resources section of my website. There is lots of help out there which can give you additional support as you work through what is behind your thoughts.

Self harm

Self harm is a relatively new disorder and has become common among teenagers. There are various reasons why people find it helpful:

- **When there is a lot of unresolved emotional or mental pain.** When you hurt your body, your brain releases a feel good hormone and for a few moments everything feels okay. Your thoughts get temporarily diverted by the physical pain too so it distracts the mind from your mental pain.

- **When you find it hard to get in touch with your feelings.** Perhaps you feel dead inside, shut down or depressed. The pain allows you to feel more alive for a few moments.
- **When you feel a lot of self hatred.** Perhaps you hate yourself, or maybe you hate your body or part of your body. Self harm is like a kind of self attack, a punishment.
- **As a cry for help** – Perhaps you don't feel as if anyone is taking your mental health problem seriously and you feel really desperate and don't know what to do. Self harm can be a way of getting friends and other people around you to see your pain.

➤ ***Whatever the reason, the relief gained from self harm is very temporary and is NOT the answer. Your scars will stay with you for the rest of your life. It's better to get to the bottom of what is going on for you.***

So, ask yourself what your self harm might be about. Do you have a lot of emotional or mental pain? What is causing this pain? Do you struggle to feel your emotions? Are you depressed? Do you hate yourself or your body? Why don't you like yourself? Ask yourself the questions in Box 14. Look at your wallpaper and dig deep to find your defective thinking.

Eating disorders

Eating disorders include phobias or anxiety about food, restrictive or controlled eating, binge or comfort eating, and anorexia and bulimia.

Again, all of these will be symptoms of how we think or feel about ourselves. Here are some suggestions about what could be at their root:

- **Control.** If we feel very out of control of lots of other aspects of our life then it's one area we CAN control.
- **Self hatred.** If you hate yourself you won't want to nourish yourself. You might also be trying to make yourself as small as possible because you don't feel as if you deserve to be here.

- **Body image.** It's easy to get obsessed with having a perfect body. If you feel as if you are bigger or less attractive or even less loveable than others then you might start controlling what you are eating.
- **Emotional eating.** If we feel lonely and empty or have a lot of undealt with emotions and negative feelings towards ourselves, we can use food as emotional comfort. This can make us eat too much. Some people will then feel guilty or disgusted with themselves which can lead to stuff like bulimia.
- **Anxiety.** If you have a lot of unresolved emotions, or feel anxious, overwhelmed or that you are resisting something, it can be hard to eat. Your stomach will clamp up and you will lose your appetite. Remember, if you are in fight or fight then your body will not prioritise digestion.
- **Phobias.** You can have phobic feelings around certain foods, textures or tastes. Your throat might feel like it's closing up and you can't swallow. What can't you swallow in life? What is being forced on you?
- **Obsessive behaviours.** If you have a lot of anxiety you can get stuck in patterns of obsessive behaviours with food. The behaviour is a ritual which helps to soothe the obsessive thoughts and feelings.
- **Patterns from early childhood.** Sometimes there are patterns from early childhood with food. For example, having food forced on you if you wouldn't eat. Parents can be very anxious around food.
- **Learnt behaviours.** A lot of adults (especially women) have very dysfunctional relationships with food as there is pressure to be slim. It's easy to pick up these anxieties and habits from a parent or older sibling.

You will need to find the individual cause of your eating disorder. What might be behind your issue? What is happening in your house around food that might be a problem? How do you feel about yourself and your body? How do you deal with your emotions? What are your feelings around food? What does food represent for you? Are you too stressed to eat?

Ask yourself the questions in Box 14. Dig into your answers and look at your wallpaper. What defective thinking or beliefs are behind all of this?

Addictions

Our brain is designed to reward us when we do things that give us pleasure. It does this by releasing chemicals that make us feel good.

Throughout the course of the day you will experience this feeling of reward many times, even when you are just doing normal activities. There will be lots of things that you are mildly addicted to that give you this feeling of reward – stuff like checking your social media account, having a sugary snack, or playing your favourite video game.

All of this is fine unless it gets out of control. If you are constantly looking for things that give you this feeling then it's probably a substitute for something that is missing in your life or for something that you don't want to feel. I call this 'filling a hole' or 'covering something up'. Let's look at each of these in turn:

- **Filling a hole.** If you feel worthless, unloved or hopeless then you will feel very flat and empty a lot of the time. You then fill this emptiness with an addictive behaviour. All the time you are absorbed in this behaviour your brain will be producing feel-good chemicals and you will feel better. But the minute you stop, you have to feel the empty feeling again. People that are depressed often have addictive behaviours.
- **Covering something up.** If you have a lot of emotional pain, perhaps from a trauma or because you repress your emotions, then you won't want to feel the pain. You avoid the pain by distracting yourself with an addictive behaviour. Again it makes you feel good temporarily and distracts you from what you don't want to feel.

So if you notice that there is something you are addicted to, even if it seems fairly harmless, ask yourself what is going on. Are you filling a hole or covering something up? What is behind your behaviour? Do you feel worthless and unloved? What untrue story are you telling yourself? What unresolved trauma are you burying? What feeling don't you want to ever feel again? Use the questions in Box 14.

➤ ***It will serve you well to get on top of any addictions while you are still young and before they get out of control. Many adults get stuck in terrible patterns of addiction with stuff like alcohol or drugs and it really destroys their lives.***

Body dysmorphia

Body dysmorphia is when you become obsessed that some part of your body or appearance is flawed. You will feel very ashamed and will want to hide this part of yourself at all costs. This can make you feel very anxious about being seen by other people, especially your peer group.

This is a complex disorder and you will need to get some professional help and support. But, remember, deep down it's really only a bunch of symptoms with a big fancy label. And all of these symptoms are being caused by your own thoughts, feelings, beliefs and perceptions.

Break the condition down into symptoms. Forget the label, put it on one side for now. Ask yourself instead what you actually suffer from? Is it anxiety? Fear? Shame? Lack of confidence? Obsessive thoughts? Read the bit about each of these conditions in this section. This will help you to understand your disorder better.

Dig into your wallpaper. Ask yourself the questions in Box 14. Try and work out why you have made this decision about your body. What happened to bring it on? Did someone say something to you? Did you have a trauma? Why are you judging yourself so harshly? What has made you reject yourself or parts of yourself so strongly? What do you wrongly believe about yourself? Why are you so worried about what others think?

You might also want to do some work on your emotions. Are you scared of feeling strong emotions? Is the body dysmorphia really all about not wanting to feel your deepest pain? Do your feelings about your body in some way represent these repressed emotions?

CHAPTER 3

Other teenage issues

In this chapter we are going to look at some other stuff that can affect our happiness. These issues don't have big names or labels but they can affect us just as much. Again, they are all symptoms of dysfunctional thinking.

Lack of confidence

Many teens suffer from a lack of confidence. Adults do too. It's probably one of the most common issues out there.

Confidence is a kind of outward expression of ourselves and our actions in the world. If we have a good sense of self worth then we will be naturally confident. We will show ourselves fully to the world without any filters. Young children usually do this. They don't doubt themselves or worry about what others think and they are totally and confidently themselves.

So why do we lose our confidence?

As we already know, as we grow up we have all kinds of experiences and we often form negative opinions about ourselves. Our self worth often takes a hit and this means that we no longer feel comfortable about putting ourselves out there in an honest and open way.

There may be parts of ourselves that we want to hide, or we may fear that we might fail, or be rejected, judged or even attacked. And so we change our behaviour, shutting ourselves down a bit, avoiding certain situations, not doing some of the things that we would have done before.

This usually peaks when we are teenagers. We have lost our small child confidence, have gained lots of negative stuff but have not yet had time to learn adult strategies for being more confident.

So ask yourself what happened to you. Why did you lose your natural confidence? What is going on in your wallpaper?

You will also need to work at pushing yourself out of your comfort zone. This is what adults have to do, we have no choice. It can feel uncomfortable but each time you succeed your confidence will grow.

➤ ***Ultimately, confidence is about getting back in touch with your true self. If you can let this shine out and stop worrying about what others think, you can be an amazing role model for other less confident people.***

Self hatred

Hating yourself is the complete opposite to what you actually should be doing. You should be loving yourself! Hate is very destructive and pointless and you need to get to the bottom of it as soon as possible.

Ask yourself why you hate yourself. Say "I hate myself because..." and find as many things as possible. Then sit and really feel all the feelings that are coming up, using the BAE technique. This will help to calm your emotions down so you can be more open to changing how you feel.

You will then need to look into your wallpaper to work out why you don't love, or even like, yourself. There will probably be some very defective thinking going on, as well as lots of limiting beliefs and untrue stories.

You can also make a list of things that you DO like about yourself. What are your gifts? What are you good at? What do other people like about you? Try and look beyond all your perceived 'faults' to your true self.

It is really important that you start learning to love yourself – probably the most important thing you'll ever do in your life. Start working on it now.

Overwhelm

Overwhelm makes us feel flustered and stressed. There is a feeling of 'too much' and we feel as if we might lose control or that we won't cope.

There are a few reasons why we get overwhelmed. On a practical level, it might be showing you that you are doing too much or that you are not organising yourself well. Are there any changes you can make?

You will also feel more easily overwhelmed if you feel as if you are not enough in some way. Why don't you feel capable? Why do you feel weak and vulnerable? Are these things really true? When did you decide this and why? How can you learn to feel stronger and more capable?

Another reason we get overwhelmed is resistance. When we decide that something is too big, too loud, too scary, too unpleasant, we resist it. By resisting it I mean we don't want to FEEL it. We try and hold it off and our mind and body goes tight against it. Unfortunately doing this makes it feel EVEN BIGGER as it gives it more energy, just like with emotions.

Next time something feels overwhelming, notice what you are resisting. What don't you want to experience or feel? What emotions are you resisting? Then just allow yourself to feel it and allow it to fill your whole body and all your senses, without any judgement. Use the BAE technique.

➤ ***Many people who feel easily overwhelmed say it is because they are sensitive. This may well be true but perhaps your sensitivity is also partly being caused by that fact that you are constantly resisting things. This makes everything feel more overwhelming and then it's easy to decide that you are really sensitive. You then create a whole persona out of this!***

Identity issues

Some of us really struggle with our identity. We often know what or who we DON'T want to be, but not who we really are.

Have another look at the chapter in Section 1 on trying to be like everyone else as this will help you remember that we are supposed to all be different. Get in touch with who you are and what your gifts are. You could even get a Human Design reading.

It's also helpful to explore what might be behind this feeling of not knowing who you are. It can come from how you were parented. If one or both of your parents were very strict, or put a lot of attention on you being perfect or good all the time, then all your attention would have been on pleasing them rather than being yourself. Or perhaps you were always comparing yourself with a sibling and focusing on competing with them rather than just being yourself?

➤ ***Some people have a much stronger sense of themselves as soon as they are born. In Human Design, some of us have a very fixed way of being while others are softer and more open. If you are more open then it is easier to get conditioned by others and also harder to get a sense of who you really are.***

It can also be helpful to ask yourself why is it so important to have an identity. Why can't you accept yourself exactly as you are RIGHT NOW. Think of your true self, who is absolutely perfect and doesn't need to be, do or change anything. What are you trying to avoid or what hole are you trying to fill by having an identity? Can you just BE instead?

Gender issues ♀♂+?

Gender is not a clearly defined thing. Imagine drawing a line with 'female' at one end and 'male' at the other. We are all somewhere on this line. We will range from not being very defined by a gender if we are around the centre of the line, to being really feminine or masculine if we are closer to one end of the line. There is no right or wrong and we are all different.

Unfortunately there is still some pressure from society for girls to be soft and caring and for boys to be tough and strong. It can be difficult if you don't conform to this view.

Perhaps you are a girl but you hate all things feminine. See if you can work out why. What is your mother's attitude towards it? What does femininity mean to you? Can you find your own unique way of expressing yourself?

Look for a role model – someone who really rocks being a woman but in a less conventional way.

Perhaps you are a boy and you don't feel as manly as other boys? Again, start by asking yourself why this is a problem? Why do you need to be strong and tough? Then look for a role model who you respect – someone who isn't tough and bulging with muscles but is perhaps sensitive, or talented or funny instead? Also, seek out like-minded friends or, if you find it really difficult to fit in with boys, find some female friends.

➤ ***The good news is that adults don't have these same expectations about men. Women actually LIKE men who are vulnerable and talk about their feelings and a lot of us really don't rate muscles that much!***

Some people can feel as if they are the wrong gender. If you have felt like this for most of your life, then a sex change can be a good option. However, if you have started questioning your gender more recently because you feel lost and unhappy and you think that creating a new identity will make you happy again, then BE CAREFUL. It's really important to explore what is behind this before taking any action. Although a sex change might be the right thing for you, it won't necessarily fix all your underlying mental health problems.

➤ ***If you are not happy in one gender, you probably won't be happy in another. Address the core issue of why you are not happy before you do anything radical to your body.***

Sexual identity

Do you have issues around your sexuality? Are you unsure whether you are straight, gay, bisexual (or any of the other identities that exist now).

At your stage of life, even though it might feel really important, there's plenty of time to experiment so don't feel any pressure to make a decision. You will get clearer over time about what feels right for you.

Again, it's all about being comfortable with yourself. Whether you are bisexual, or straight but attracted to very feminine boys or very masculine girls, or just attracted to certain people and gender is not relevant, just follow your joy. There is no right or wrong.

If your sexuality is a big deal to you, look at your wallpaper. Why are you doubting yourself? Why does it matter so much? Who are you trying to please? Are you worrying too much about what others think? Work on your self esteem and on being comfortable being you. The more comfortable you are in yourself, the less bothered your peer group will be about who you want to have sex with!

Many teenagers worry about telling their parents that they are gay. Most parents are okay about it but, unfortunately, it can sometimes take some of them a bit of time to get used to the idea. If one of your parents is really against it, this is their problem and to do with their issues, limitations and fears, not yours. The main thing is not to make yourself wrong and to stay true to yourself.

Insecurity about your looks or body

Body image is a HUGE thing now. The media, especially social media, focuses a lot on how we look. There's an ideal size, shape and look and young people are generally very judgmental about how others look.

Most of us don't conform to this ideal look and everyone has their own unique beauty (just as we all have our own unique personalities and traits).

➤ ***I took my daughter to a theatre audition once. They were auditioning for extras in a film and were looking for a certain look. They lined up three children at a time and photographed them. I started looking at the children in a different way. If I was a casting director who would I pick? Who had a good look? I was amazed at how conventional attractiveness no longer held any interest. I was looking instead for character, interesting features, things that stood out. The conventionally pretty ones suddenly looked really bland and ordinary.***

Look in a mirror and have a look at yourself without the filter of that bland and boring conventional look. What do you like about yourself? Is there one feature of your face or body that is especially interesting or eye catching? If you find this hard then ask a friend or a parent to help. They will spot things straight away. And it may not be an obvious thing that you see in the mirror. You may have a nice walk or your body language might be attractive, or you might have a beautiful smile.

The more you can seek out and appreciate your good points and stop focusing on where you lack the better. Go for a walk and look at as many old people as possible. Then go home and look at yourself in the mirror. Appreciate your young fresh skin, the clear whites of your eyes, your white teeth, your strong smooth body. These things won't last forever and to older people ALL young people look beautiful!

True beauty comes from the inside rather than the outside. Have a look at people at school. Find someone who is a lovely happy person who is not obviously conventionally attractive. Then find someone who is very pretty or good looking but perhaps a bit bitchy or scowly. Being really attractive isn't everything. Self confidence and inner happiness gives you a glow that shines right out of you and affects how others feel about you.

➤ ***And remember, some people ARE more attractive than others. Perhaps that's their thing, one of their gifts. Be okay with that.***

If you are still struggling with how you look, examine your wallpaper and see why you are so down on yourself. Where did it come from? Why is it so important for you to look a certain way? Dig deep and see if you can find the root of the problem.

Insecurity about your personality or abilities

A lot of teenagers think that there's something wrong with them – that they are boring, shy, stupid, useless, etc. We make these judgements about ourselves from quite a young age and they can be difficult to change.

But I can promise you, there is absolutely NOTHING wrong with you, it's just your perception. If you don't believe me, ask other people. They will all agree with me.

Again, you will need to look at your wallpaper to get to the bottom of this. Are you trying to be like everyone else and focusing on where you think you lack? Have you made up an untrue story about yourself? Remember, we are all different and we all have different gifts, and that's GOOD.

Feeling like you don't fit in or are too different

If you feel as if you just don't fit in or that you are very different to everyone else, ask yourself how true this is at a deep level. How much of this is just a story you have created? Have a look at your wallpaper. What are you thinking, feeling or doing that might be creating this?

As we are all different it may well be true that you ARE a little more unusual and that fitting in IS harder for you. But that doesn't mean you'll never fit in anywhere. You just haven't met the right people yet.

In the meantime, the best thing to do is to just concentrate on being you. If you feel bad about yourself and are trying to hide parts of yourself or to act differently from who you really are then you will probably come across as being awkward, unfriendly or uncomfortable. If you are comfortable in your own skin then other people are much more likely to like you.

Feeling unloved or unloveable

If you feel as if you aren't very loveable, it's probably because you don't like yourself very much. We are all very sensitive to how others feel about themselves. If you have rejected yourself then others will be inclined do the same. Ask yourself why are you rejecting yourself.

It could also be that this is just a story you have made up about yourself and that actually everyone DOES like you. See if you can work out whether there might be some truth to this and ask yourself why you have created this untrue story.

We are all different and on the surface some of us are naturally more 'loveable' than others. Perhaps that's their gift. Be okay with who you are. The more you get in touch with and feel comfortable with your authentic self, the more people will like you. And if you really like yourself it won't matter so much what others think.

Some people feel unloved by their parents and they then grow up feeling as if they are unloveable. Our parents usually DO love us but sometimes they are struggling with their own mental health. It is difficult to love others when you don't love yourself. Know that you ARE loveable, however your parents treated you. Going forwards, you will need to find a way of loving yourself from within. Do lots of tapping on yourself and it would also be really helpful to get back in touch with your true self.

Difficult relationships with parents and siblings

Many teenagers have difficult relationships with their parents. Parenting is hard and parents often get stuck in old ways of dealing with things, using techniques that worked really well when you were five but just don't work any longer. You can get frustrated because you don't feel respected and understood and your parents feel frustrated because they don't feel like they are in control of you any more.

Try and have a grown up conversation with them. Find a time when everyone is in a good mood. Explain how frustrated you feel and ask them if there is another way of doing things. Don't make it about blame and anger, try and stay calm. Hopefully they will be open to listening to you and between you you can find some creative solutions.

As everyone is different, not all parents will want to or be able to do this. They might also need a bit of time and space to make changes.

➤ ***If you don't feel as if they are willing to listen to you or take you seriously then try writing it to them. This will give you time to consider all your points carefully and communicate them in a clear way.***

It's good to look at your behaviour too rather than just blaming your parents. Is there something YOU can change? Can you react in a different way? What are the things that are most important to your parents? Can you make more of an effort with these? Could you ask them to do something differently for you in exchange? Sometimes it's about compromise ("If you do ... for me, I will do ... for you").

Relationships with brothers and sisters can also be difficult. Try talking to them to see if you can sort things out in a more grown up way. If they aren't interested in doing that then, again, look at your own behaviour. Is there anything you can do differently that will change the patterns?

➤ ***It's amazing how one person changing allows others to change. Try it and see what happens.***

If you feel as if one of your siblings is more important or more lovable than you then you will need to look at your wallpaper. Although some people do seem easier to love at a surface level, deep down NO-ONE is more important or more lovable than anyone else. Look at where this untrue belief came from, when you created it and what wrong thinking is behind it.

Problems with friendships

Relationships with friends can be very tricky. As a teenager, it will be very important to you to be accepted by your peer group and having friends is a big part of this. It makes you feel good when you have close friendships. As human beings we all seek this kind of connection.

If you are struggling to make or keep friends, look at the problem from a distance. What is going on? Why does the same thing keep happening over and over again? Rather than blaming other people, look at your own behaviour. Are you too needy, too aloof, too outspoken, too emotional? Is this really how you are or are you being triggered?

Look at what is going on in your wallpaper. How is your inner world affecting how others feel about you? How much do you like yourself (remember, if you really like yourself then it's much easier for others to like you)? Are you insecure? Are you dealing with your emotions badly?

It might be that you just have the wrong friends. Perhaps you are always arguing with them, or they are not very kind or supportive, or maybe you just feel as if you don't have much in common with them any more.

Extract yourself from friendships carefully and kindly. You can either let things gradually drift – ie stay friendly but start building new friendships. Or just have a really honest conversation. You can say something like "I really like you but I feel as if we don't have much in common any more", or "I feel unhappy with all the arguing and drama between us". Don't blame them or make any personal comments about them as a person. Remember that a friendship is a two way thing and any problems can be as much about you as about them.

If you find it hard to make any friends at all, then perhaps this is not the right time for you. As you specialise more in the subjects you really enjoy at school you will meet more like-minded people and it will be easier to make friends. Don't put pressure on yourself and don't reject yourself.

➤ ***It's very common to have friendship issues as a teenager and I know many people who didn't have friends until they were adults. Be grateful for your family and know that a good friendship is coming your way.***

Problems with dating

Many of you, especially if you are an older teenager, will be starting to date. This is full of all sorts of problems as relationships will act as triggers for all the stuff in your wallpaper. If you feel worthless and unloveable, or are not dealing with your emotions well then this will DEFINITELY all play out in your relationships!

You may notice that some of the issues you have been having with your family and friends crop up in your relationships. If this happens then it really is a wake up call that it's something that is coming from you!

If you are having problems with relationships, rather than blaming the other person, see what is going on in your wallpaper. The more you improve this, the easier your relationships will be.

Here are some tips to help you with some common relationship problems:

- **"I can't get a boyfriend/girlfriend".** If you lack confidence and find it hard to get into a relationship, work on your self confidence and self esteem first. Learn to love yourself more. Be comfortable in your own skin. Be friendly, smiley and happy and show interest in other people. It will happen once you are more relaxed and happy in yourself.

- **"I always choose the wrong person".** We often choose partners who give us something we lack in ourselves. So, if we are fearful, we might choose a partner who is very controlling as they make us feel safe. We also often pick a partner who is like one of our parents in some way, because it feels familiar. Next time you are looking for a partner, think carefully about what you REALLY want.
- **"I'm worried they will leave me".** Once you've found that special someone, you can end up putting a lot of pressure on yourself to be really perfect all the time so they don't leave you. Have a look at what might be going on in your wallpaper and see if there is something behind this. It's best to just be yourself. If they don't like you for who you are then it's good to find out quickly.
- **"My partner is being abusive".** If you are with someone who is abusive to you in any way (physically or mentally) it is best to get out as soon as possible. If you don't, they will chip away at your self esteem and it will get harder and harder to leave. Ask yourself why you are allowing someone to be so disrespectful to you. What's behind this?
- **"I'm being cheated on".** If someone cheats on you then, again, it is best to leave. Generally people are either faithful or they are not and, if it's happened once, it'll probably happen again. Don't allow people to treat you so disrespectfully. If it keeps happening, ask yourself whether you are choosing the wrong sort of people. Are you always going for the popular, good looking boys who can get any girl, for example?
- **"My partner is trying to change me".** Once you are in a relationship, just be yourself. If the other person tries to change you then stand your ground. DON'T EVER CHANGE YOURSELF FOR ANYONE ELSE. Remember, the right person will love you exactly as you are.
- **"I know I need to leave but...".** It can be hard to end relationships, even if they are making us unhappy. We often end up waiting for the next person to come along first. This is not a good idea as it can cause a lot

of hurt. Also, it is good to have some time to yourself between relationships as it will help you to get clearer about who you are and what you want.

Exam pressure

Exams are a well-known cause of stress. But why do some people get really stressed and others don't? Some of us are obviously better at academic work, or more organised, or more self disciplined, but the level of stress is not necessarily related to how smart people are or how good at exams they are.

The difference is PERCEPTION. The main reasons why teenagers get stressed over exams is that they are putting pressure on themselves not to fail. Why is it so important not to fail? Are you worried about what others will think? Are your parents really strict and make you feel as if they won't love you if you don't do well? Are you down on yourself and need to do well at exams to feel good? Do you feel as if you always have to be perfect? See if you can work out why it's so important to do well.

The best way to handle exams is to work hard and then do your best on the day. If you don't do very well then you know you did everything you should have done and that maybe academic exams isn't your thing. Plenty of people leave school without good grades and end up living a happy and fulfilling life. Don't make your exam results define your self worth.

➛ ***If you get really stressed before an exam, do some tapping on yourself. The power pose will help too (see Box 5 on page 57).***

Bullying

Bullying is usually not as blatant as it used to be as schools have worked hard to stamp it out. Unfortunately this means that it has gone under cover and has become more subtle and psychological.

Bullying often takes place among friendship groups or with other people you are in regular contact with. It's also very common on social media. Bullying can vary from ongoing subtle digs to big attacks.

Girls and boys tend to bully in different ways. Boys usually use banter, putting you down as much as they can in a jokey but rude way. If you get upset they tell you not to be so soft and that they are only joking. It's almost like a macho thing to see how tough you are.

Girls can be very devious with bullying. It can include things like constantly putting you down in small and subtle ways, leaving you out, power struggles, talking about you behind your back and turning other people against you.

Bullies seek out people who seem weak and sensitive, who will react and be upset and who won't retaliate. They do it to make themselves feel more powerful. If being bullied is a theme in your life then ask yourself what is going on in your wallpaper. Why are you coming across as an easy target? Why do other people's comments affect you so much? Remember, you can't change what people say to you but you CAN change how you react.

It's good to take some action against the bullying as this will give out a message that you are not weak and powerless. If you are being bullied by a friend, try talking to them about it. Let them know how you feel as they may not be meaning to be unkind. If it continues, find new friends.

➤ ***Even if you have to be alone for a while, this is better than being bullied as it can damage your self esteem for the rest of your life***

If you are being bullied on social media, then unfollow people who don't make you feel good. Make your social media environment a good supportive one with fewer people (if you need to have lots of followers to make you feel good then have a look at what is going on in your wallpaper!). If things are really bad then take a complete break from social media and return to it when you are in a happier place.

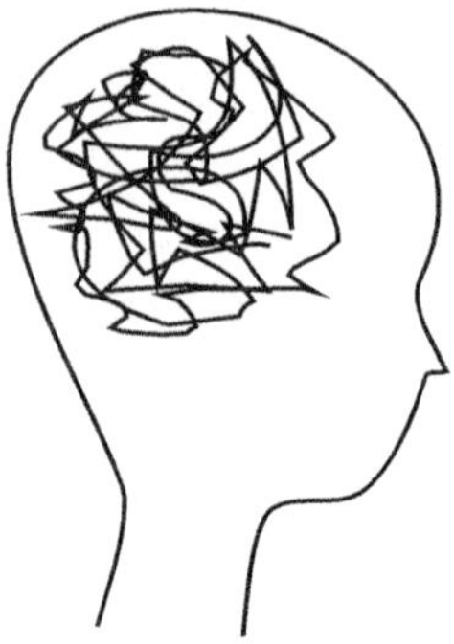

CHAPTER 4

Brain wiring

In this final chapter we are going to look at things like autism, Aspergers, ADD, ADHD, dyslexia and dyspraxia.

Of course none of the above are mental health issues but they can often lead to mental health issues because of how they make you feel about yourself.

Embrace your difference

Whether you are on the spectrum (autism or Aspergers) or have other issues such as ADD, ADHD, dyslexia or dyspraxia, you may have challenges with a things like social skills, handling emotions, communication, concentration, reading and writing, planning, organising, thinking etc. Your brain is wired a little differently and life might be a bit tougher for you, especially at school.

It might feel difficult to do all the 'normal' social stuff that other teenagers do and you may worry that you just aren't going to cope with life. It can also make you feel as if you are defective in some way and that can make you feel ashamed or that you aren't good enough. Reactions can range from giving up on yourself and getting depressed to becoming a super high achiever to prove that you are as good as everyone else.

But it's really important that you don't give up on yourself or stress yourself out trying to constantly prove yourself. Every one of you will have different challenges but you will also all have unique gifts and abilities. Your difference is very important to society and you will bring something that other people can't. See yourself as UNIQUE rather than defective.

Most of the biggest innovations and inventions have come from people on the autistic spectrum – Einstein, Darwin, Bill Gates, Steve Jobs, Mozart, Isaac Newton, to name a few.

➤ ***If it wasn't for the autistic gene we would probably still all be hunter gatherers sitting around the camp fire!***

There are also many other famous people in history who were dyslexic or dyspraxic or who had ADD or ADHD – Alexander Graham Bell, Leonardo de Vinci, Thomas Edison, Henry Ford, Picasso, Muhammad Ali. If you don't know who these people are then Google them! And you will all know who Greta Thunberg is. She is a total inspiration.

The main thing is to stop thinking that everyone needs to be the same and focusing on all the areas you feel you are lacking otherwise you will never be happy with who you are. Focus on what you CAN do rather than what you CAN'T do so that you can start to appreciate and develop your uniqueness.

Finding your strengths

There are generally three different ways of thinking and we usually have a combination of these. However, if you are autistic or have Aspergers or any of the other syndromes mentioned in this section, you may find that you favour one of them more strongly:

- **Visual thinkers.** You will think in pictures and have to see things, either in your mind or physically, to process information. You may have a photographic memory.
- **Verbal/logical thinkers.** You will be good with words and can learn languages easily. You will enjoy making lists and memorising things. You will have a huge memory for verbal facts.

- **Pattern thinkers.** You will think in patterns so will be good at finding meaningful patterns in data. You will be good at stuff like maths.

Which type of thinker do you think you might be? Can you start looking for opportunities to use this way of thinking more? Develop it with hobbies and things you love doing and, as you get older, you will have the potential to be a very useful employee.

Look for other strengths that you have too. Perhaps you are a creative and original thinker, a strategic problem solver, or good at spotting patterns and solving problems? If you can't see your own strengths then ask other people who know you well.

Google stuff like "What are autistic people good at" or "What are people with dyspraxia good at", "What careers suit people with ADHD" etc. There's lots of positive stuff out there to get you thinking.

Getting a diagnosis ✓

Some of you may be reading this section and suspecting that you might be mildly on the spectrum but have never been tested or diagnosed. Perhaps you have always felt like you are very different to other people, or you struggle with some of the things others seem to manage easily? This can make you really down on yourself.

Although I don't think labels are always useful, it can be helpful to get a formal diagnosis. One of the biggest advantages of doing this is that there is a lot of specialist help around, especially at school. This can help make your life a bit easier.

I think you have to ask yourself whether having a label will make you feel better or worse. If you are already down on yourself because you feel as if you are a bit different, ask yourself whether it would be a relief to know there is a reason for it, or would it make you feel even worse?

➤ ***And remember, you are still YOU whether you have a diagnosis or not so what really matters is how you feel about yourself deep down.***

Girls and autism ♀

Boys are four times more likely to get a diagnosis than girls and they tend to get diagnosed when they are very young. However, the average age for a girl to get diagnosed is 16! This means that there are quite a few younger teenage girls with undiagnosed mild autism or other wiring stuff.

The reason that girls don't get diagnosed so easily is that they are much better at something called 'masking'. Masking is where we hide things and learn to act in a certain way. Girls tend to be more self aware and are more conscious of fitting in with others so they tend to be good at copying how other people are behaving. This means they can often appear very sociable. However, as they get older and relationships get more complex, they can start to struggle.

There are many symptoms of autism in girls and everyone will have slightly different ones, but here is a list of some of the common ones:

- Relying on copying other people's behaviour to fit in.
- Being unusually sensitive to things like bright lights, crowds, noise, strong smells, certain textures (including food).
- Being extremely ticklish.
- Find it hard to make eye contact.
- Having emotional meltdowns when frustrated.
- Suffering from depression, anxiety and moodiness.
- Finding it hard to make and to keep friends.
- Being quiet, shy and passive.
- A strong almost obsessive interest in one thing and conversations being restricted to this thing.
- Liking routines and structures.
- Being rigid and detail-orientated.
- Creating a vivid and complicated fantasy world.
- Feeling like you don't know how to be yourself.

All the above symptoms can also occur in non-autistic people so if you have a few of them it may not mean anything. But it may be worth considering getting a diagnosis if you have a lot of these traits.

Accepting yourself

For those of you who have been diagnosed with a spectrum disorder of any kind, your biggest enemy is yourself. Listen to your inner talk about yourself. Is it positive? If not, work on changing it.

➤ ***Channel your inner Greta Thunberg. She has discovered the positive benefits of her Aspergers and she really rocks it.***

Life will get easier for you when you are an adult. You can choose who you spend your time with, you will find a job suited to your unique skills and life will generally feel more in your control.

If you have been really down on yourself for many years because of your wiring, then look at what damage your feelings about it has done to your wallpaper and to how you feel about yourself. You can't change your symptoms but you can definitely change how you feel about them.

If you can accept your wiring and learn to work around it and make it into a gift then there's no reason why you shouldn't have as happy a life as anyone else. If you spend the whole time hating it, fighting against it and feeling like a failure then your life will always be difficult and miserable.

SECTION 9

Lifestyle factors

CHAPTER 1

Nutrition and diet

This book doesn't feel complete without some information about diet, exercise and other physical stuff. Let's start by looking at diet as nutrition can play an important part in our mental health.

How diet affects mental health

In the last 50 years there has been a MASSIVE rise in pre-prepared meals and junk food. Many children are brought up on a diet of pizzas, burgers, pasta, fishfingers, crisps, biscuits, sweets and sugary drinks.

We all know that junk food is bad for our bodies, but what about our mental health? Our diet plays a bigger role in how we feel mentally than we might think. Here are some ways in which is can affect us:

- **Nutrients.** Our bodies and our minds need lots of different nutrients to stay calm and balanced. Junk food is low in nutrients as it is based on cheap ingredients. Many of the nutrients it does contain are often lost in the preparation, cooking and storing processes.
- **Inflammation.** Junk food is very high in processed vegetable oils. Our bodies don't like these and they can cause something called 'inflammation', which is where our immune system switches on to try and get rid of them. Inflammation has been linked to depression.

- **Poor digestion.** Eating poor quality food can upset your digestion. This means that it will be harder to absorb nutrients.
- **Toxic load.** Junk food is high in salt, sugar, fat, sweeteners, hormones and pesticides, which can all overload the liver. An overworked liver will affect your mental health, making it harder to concentrate, depleting your energy and making you more angry and impatient. It can also cause depression.
- **Sugar.** The body uses nutrients from other food to break down sugar. In particular, it uses magnesium and B vitamins, both of which are also very important for calming you down. This means if you are eating a lot of sugar, you will find it harder to relax. Sugar also disrupts your blood sugar, giving you highs and lows which will affect your mood and energy.
- **Calories.** Junk food has been designed to be very tasty and so it is easy to eat too much. If you have a tendency towards comfort eating then it will be easy to put weight on. This can affect your confidence.

Healthy eating

So, what should you be eating?

In an ideal world you would be eating healthy home cooked meals. It might seem a big deal but it's not that hard to do. It's also cheaper than buying junk food and takeaways.

Start by telling your parents you want to eat more healthily. They are usually happy to hear this and will probably help you with it. If they can't or don't want to, focus on the meals you have some control over, like breakfast and lunch. And cut down on unhealthy snacks and drinks.

Here are some tips for healthy eating:

- Don't eat too much junk food.
- Eat as much FRESH food as possible (meat, fish, fruit and vegetables).
- Cut down on sugar and avoid sweeteners.
- Drink water or tea rather than sweet drinks.

If it all feels a bit overwhelming then just start with some small changes. Perhaps eat one piece of fresh fruit a day, water down your fruit juice and cut out one unhealthy snack. If you want to find out more about healthy eating, there is lots of information online.

Eating healthily is good for you psychologically too. By nourishing your body better, you are treating yourself more lovingly and kindly. This will help you to feel better about yourself.

We are all different

As well as eating healthily, it is also important to make sure you are eating the right food for YOUR body.

In the past our bodies would have adapted to the local food. If you lived in Iceland, you would have eaten mainly protein (fish and meat). If you lived somewhere hot like the Caribbean, your diet would have been high in carbohydrates (fruit and vegetables). If you lived in England, your diet would have been a mix of protein and carbohydrates (meat and vegetables).

So, depending on where you have originally evolved from, your body will be better suited to a certain diet. Most of us are a mix of different DNA these days so it can be hard to know your origins. There's a book called *The Metabolic Typing Diet* which has a useful quiz that helps you work out whether you are a protein eater, a carbohydrate eater or a mix of the two.

➤ ***Children have a good sense of what food suits them best. My friend's son has always really liked meat, right from a young age. He is pale skinned and probably had some northern European origins. Another child I know loves fruit. Her grandfather is from Iraq.***

So go with your instincts. If you feel really drawn to meat and protein then make sure you have a fair amount in your diet. If you are darker skinned then perhaps you would benefit from more fruit and vegetables.

And listen to your body. Do you feel bloated and tired when you eat certain foods? Is the food you are eating making you feel full or do you feel hungry quickly? Try and eat things that make your body feel good.

Taking supplements

If your mental health is very poor and your diet is not as good as it could be, take some vitamin supplements. These should not replace a healthy diet but they are a useful way to get back on track.

The following vitamins are very important for good mental health:

- **Magnesium** is needed for over 1,000 chemical reactions in the body. If we don't have enough our flight and flight hormones get more easily triggered. It also calms the nervous system and helps us get back in a parasympathetic resting state. If you are a stressy person you will definitely need a good supply of magnesium. It is hard to absorb so I thoroughly recommend a product called ReMag. There are cheaper ones around but it will last a couple of months and is worth every penny.
- **B vitamins** are also important for keeping us calm and balanced. They help our energy levels and are also involved in the production of brain chemicals which control our mood. Deficiencies have been linked to anxiety and depression so if you get stressed or depressed, take some good quality high-dose supplements.
- **Vitamin D** is important for our immune system and for preventing anxiety and depression. It's only activated when we get the sun on our skin so, unless you spend a lot of time outdoors, it might be a good idea to take a supplement.
- **Omega 3** also has a good effect on our stress levels as it balances out unhealthy oils and reduces inflammation (and inflammation can lead to depression). It's difficult to get enough in your diet unless you eat oily fish. As many of you don't like fish, it's easier to take a supplement.
- **Iron** can also affect your mood. This is one of the most common deficiencies, especially among women. A good supplement to take is Floradix as it is gentle on your stomach and has other vitamins in too.

There is lots of advice online about supplements or you can speak to your GP or local health food shop if you want more information.

CHAPTER 2

Body matters

As well as being aware of what we put INTO our bodies, it's also important to consider how we USE our bodies. Let's start by looking at exercise.

Exercise

Our bodies have evolved to run and walk, to stretch and twist, to jump and crouch. When we were hunter gatherers we would have had strong and agile bodies. If we were weak and unfit we would not have survived.

Today you probably spend most of the time sitting or lying down – watching TV, on your phone or other devices, reading, sitting in classrooms, doing homework, lying in bed. Not only does this affect your body but it also affects your mind.

Exercise is probably one of the most important ways to improve mental health. When we exercise, it helps us to burn up stress hormones and to release feel-good chemicals that improve our mood. It also takes us out of our heads and thoughts and more into our bodies which makes us feel happier and more relaxed. If the mind isn't churning out stressful thoughts then the body will automatically relax. And when the body is relaxed, this will help to relax the mind. Remember the feedback loop of mind to body and body back to mind?

Exercise is good for good our hearts, blood vessels, liver, kidneys, skin and digestion. It also helps us to keep our hormones in balance, release pent up emotions, break down toxins, reduce inflammation, burn up excess calories and build muscle and strength.

Nowadays we have to build exercise into our daily routine otherwise it just doesn't happen. This takes a bit of effort and willpower and many people just can't be bothered or don't have time.

➤ ***Is this you? Do you spend most of the day curled over your phone or slumped on a chair, bed or sofa?***

Ask yourself why you don't exercise. After all, we all know it's good for us. Perhaps you feel depressed and hopeless, or you have given up on yourself, or you hate your body, or you feel too tired and unfit?

Ways to exercise

There are many ways to build exercise into your life. The secret is to find something you enjoy doing. If you are mentally absorbed you will hardly notice that you are doing exercise. Here are some suggestions:

- **Join a club.** For example, football, boxing, netball, swimming, judo, badminton, tennis, running, dancing, etc. Try out a few different things.
- **Go for a run.** Start with a short distance and build it up. You could ask a friend or family member to join you. Set yourself goals – work towards a local 5k run, then 10k and then even a marathon one day.
- **Join a gym.** There are lots of things you can do in a gym, like running, cycling, swimming or group classes. Try out some different things.
- **Get out on your bike.** Find a couple of friends that want to join you and cycle somewhere at the weekend that you can't walk to.
- **Find an online fitness programme.** Take part in a fitness programme or play an interactive online game. There is plenty to choose from.
- **Walking.** Build walking into your daily routine. Get a pedometer and try and do 10,000 steps a day. Walk to school if you can. Walk the dog if you have one.

Creating good habits with exercise

Remember, any exercise is better than none so start gently and build it up. Start with exercising once a week and then build it up to two or three times a week. You will notice that you feel mentally and physically better.

Because you are still young your body will get fit very quickly. It gets harder as we get older as our bodies stiffen up and our hearts, lungs and muscles get less efficient. It's good to get into the habit of having regular exercise now as it'll be good for your mind and body for your whole life.

And be careful not to go too far the other way. If you start to feel obsessed by doing exercise, perhaps focusing on losing weight or building muscle definition, ask yourself what is behind this. Why are you overweight? Why is it so important to be thin? Why do you need to look strong and defined? Have a look at your wallpaper. Remember, it's healthy to exercise but not to become obsessed with it.

Other ways to nurture your body

As well as exercise, these things will also help keep your body healthy:

- **Sunshine.** Get outside in the sunshine without sun screen (being careful not to burn). Not only will this boost your vitamin D levels which is good for your health, it will also improve your mood.
- **Good posture.** Are you always curled over your phone or peering into a computer? This can disrupt your breathing and digestion and can also give you backache, a stiff neck and headaches. Be aware of your posture as much as possible. Keep your shoulders back and relaxed, your back straight, and lift your chest slightly. Imagine there's a piece of string coming out of the top of your head and you are floating from this.
- **Sleep.** It is easy to get less than eight hours of sleep. As well as making us tired and irritable, it's also bad for our bodies and minds. Create good sleep habits – have a regular bedtime, do something relaxing beforehand, switch off your phone and other devices, and keep lighting low. If your mind is very active then listen to a relaxation exercise.

CHAPTER 3

Social media

Social media is probably such a big part of your life that you won't be able to imagine living without it.

It's hard to believe that it has only been around for the past ten years or so and is a completely new way of interacting. In fact, you are the first generation to experience it while you are growing up.

The benefits of social media

Let's start by looking at some POSITIVES of social media:

- It's fun and entertaining and stops you from being bored.
- It's useful for connecting with and keeping in touch with friends.
- It lets you connect to lots of people instantly. This can create a sense of being part of a bigger community.
- You can share problems and get support.
- It gives you a place to be heard and so you can voice your opinions.
- It's useful for raising awareness and taking action about stuff that is going on in the world.

Social media makes us feel good because every time we get a like or a positive comment or a good feeling of connection we get a little hit of a chemical called dopamine in our brain. This makes us feel happy.

But, because this happiness is very short term, we have to keep returning to get our next fix. Social media is therefore very addictive. This isn't a problem in itself – if you have good self esteem and are self disciplined then it can bring many positive things to your life.

The flip side of social media

In a recent survey of 1,000 young people, over a third said that social media made them feel anxious, sad or depressed. There is plenty of other stuff on the internet to support this too and there are increasing concerns that it's not good for our mental well being.

The thing with social media is that it's perfectly harmless in itself. If you are happy and confident then it's just a fun way of connecting with the world. But, if you have lots of negative stuff in your wallpaper, then it's a different story. Here are some of the ways that it can cause problems:

- **Outside validation**. If you need outside validation to feel good about yourself then a lack of likes can make you feel bad about yourself. You can then form beliefs about yourself such as "I am boring", "No-one likes me" or "I'm not funny/interesting/attractive".
- **Low self esteem.** If you have low self esteem or your emotions are easily triggered then it's easy to read things into people's comments that they didn't mean. You may find yourself over analysing everything.
- **Stops you being yourself.** Social media reinforces the idea that there is a perfect way of being and this stops you from really being yourself. You will always be thinking about yourself in relation to others, looking for where you think you are lacking.
- **Issues with your looks.** If you have any issues with your looks or body, social media will be a nightmare for you! You will always be comparing yourself with everyone else's aesthetically perfect photos (people only post their favourite photos). There are also lots of ads on Instagram featuring perfect models and focusing on beauty and weight loss, which doesn't help.

- **Everyone else is happy.** Social media creates the illusion that everyone is having a good time and no one has any problems. People generally only share the good stuff and they create a kind of fake story about their life. This can make you feel as if there's something wrong with you and your life.
- **Feeling excluded.** If you see pictures of parties and events that you weren't invited to then this can make you feel socially excluded and rejected. This in turn can create a sense of isolation and loneliness.
- **Stops you interacting with life.** Social media gives us a constant stream of easy and absorbing entertainment. Rather than being out in the world having experiences that help us to grow as people, we can become shut down and a bit limited, almost scared of interacting with real life.

If you feel triggered by social media, use it as an opportunity to learn something about yourself. Are you looking for outside validation? Are you comparing yourself with others and focusing on where you think you lack?

➛ ***Remember that social media isn't really the problem, your wallpaper is. All social media is doing is shining a light on your issues.***

Getting the best from social media

Social media will probably always be part of your life so it's good to get a handle on it now and to manage it so that it works well for you. So here are some tips on getting the most from social media:

- **Choose your community.** Remember that you have complete control over who you are following and who is following you. Make it a community that makes you feel good rather than focusing on getting as many followers as possible. Unfollow anyone who makes you feel unhappy in any way. Be really ruthless and have a good clear down.
- **Find good role models to follow.** There are a lot of people who post honest stuff about their mental health and how they have managed to overcome low self esteem and other issues. They are often positive and inspiring and can help you to change the way you think about your own

issues. Find people like this to follow rather than negative, opinionated, moany, bitchy, gossipy people!

- **Be yourself.** Unlike real life, you have total control over your social media account. You don't have to copy how other people do things and you can choose who you follow and what you post. Make it a place where you really enjoy being you.
- **Limit your time.** Cut down the time you spend on social media. Give yourself a daily limit and stick to it. Use the extra time free time to do something which will increase your confidence and skills.
- **Meet up with friends.** Make sure you spend plenty of time with friends in real life. And put your phone away while you are with them so that you connect properly.
- **Spot your triggers.** Use social media to help you see what is going on in your wallpaper.
- **Take a break.** If you feel as if social media is adding to your poor mental health then have a break from it. This will give you time to see whether you feel better without it and it will also help you to understand how it's affecting you. Don't go back to it until you have made some changes.

SECTION 10

How to be happy

CHAPTER 1

Reclaiming your happiness

We've covered a lot of stuff in this book. Let's summarise some the main things. See if you can spot what might be standing in the way of YOUR happiness:

- Always comparing yourself with others and focusing on where you think you are lacking rather than noticing who you REALLY are.
- Making up an untrue story about yourself, who you are, your abilities or even what you think others think of you.
- Not loving or even liking yourself, and feeling unloveable or not enough.
- Constantly being triggered by a trauma.
- Having obsessive thoughts and getting stuck in your head all the time.
- Being ruled by your emotions or constantly repressing them.
- Fearing failure and always needing to be perfect.
- Being addicted to negativity rather than seeking out happiness.
- Constantly blaming others for your negative feelings.
- Needing to be in control and resisting life when it isn't what you want.
- Being out of touch with your true self.
- Not looking after your body.

Later in this section I am going to help you to put together a personalised action plan so that you can work on letting go of all the things that are stopping you from being happy.

First, let's define what happiness actually is.

Happiness

Happiness can range from a gentle and peaceful feeling of contentment right up to exuberant and energetic joy. It's a lovely feeling which just makes everything seem okay.

➤ ***Happiness is a state rather than a trait and it can come and go. Even the happiest person isn't happy all the time and it's almost the contrast of not being happy that makes happiness feel so good.***

So what controls whether we feel happy or not? You've guessed it – your wallpaper. This is why some people are happier than others. Their wallpaper is much clearer and they know who they are, have good self esteem, handle their emotions well and flow with whatever life brings.

To feel happy our minds need to be relaxed and accepting and we need to feel safe and connected and that our life is meeting our expectations. If we are overthinking, feeling unsafe, questioning whether we are good enough, feeling dissatisfied, resisting what life is bringing us, feeling lonely or disconnected then our happiness will be blocked.

I use the word 'blocked' because I believe that happiness is not something that we have to learn or achieve or force, but is OUR NATURAL STATE. All we have to do is to work on all the stuff that is blocking it. Then happiness will naturally fill the space.

So see your level of happiness like a kind of measurement of how you are doing inside. If you are generally unhappy then you need to look at what is blocking your happiness.

Making changes

Throughout this book I've given you lots of information, ideas and exercises. Hopefully it has given you a better understanding of what is blocking you.

However, although understanding all this stuff is very important, it's not the whole story.

➤ ***You also have to TAKE ACTION!***

If you just read this book, absorb it all with your mind, put the book back down and then carry on doing exactly the same things then your mental health WILL PROBABLY NOT CHANGE.

I learnt this the hard way. I had been dabbling in all of this stuff for years. I love learning about it. I love reading books about it. I love going on courses. I love having interesting conversations about it. I know exactly what you need to do to be happy and I have all the tools to help me.

Overall my mental health was pretty good but there were a couple of big patterns that I hadn't got on top of. Also, I didn't feel as if I was living in a really vibrant and happy way. In the end it took a health issue for me to realise that if I wanted to have a really happy and healthy future then I needed to do more than just 'know' all this stuff with my mind.

I also felt like a bit of a fraud. Here I was, writing this book and telling you to make all these changes and take all these actions but I hadn't actually tried many of them out myself. How did I know they would work? The only way to be sure was to test them out.

As I'm terrible at motivating myself and have no self discipline, it felt as if it was going to be really hard work to make changes. But my health issue kept me focused and I very quickly found that I enjoyed my new practices.

I'm now about six months into it as I write this and it is definitely making a big difference. I have some days where I don't have time or I get distracted by something that seems more interesting, but I just restart again the next day as I know it is the key to having a healthy mind and body.

Here are some of the changes I've experienced:

- I feel happier.
- I feel calmer and more peaceful.
- I find it easier to relax.
- I get less emotionally triggered by other people.
- I am not as fearful.
- I am able to redirect my thoughts when they become negative.
- I notice my behaviour, seeing where I am still being triggered.
- I like myself more and am being kinder to myself.
- I feel more loving and accepting towards others.

Steps to happiness

So, what have I been doing to create these changes?

These are the main nine things:

1. **Understanding.** Although I already had a good understanding about what was going on for me, writing this book really helped to clarify it.
2. **Noticing.** I watch myself closely and notice when I am having negative thoughts, being triggered, and blaming others for my feelings.
3. **Feeling.** If any feelings come up during the day, I sit with them and really feel and accept them. I allow them to expand and fill my body.
4. **Clearing.** If anything upsets me or I feel stressed about anything, I tap on it. I also tap regularly on any ongoing deeper patterns.
5. **Connecting.** I spend time every day sitting quietly and connecting with my spiritual side and my true self.
6. **Positivity.** I focus on being the best version of myself. I try and be kind to myself and, whatever life brings, I look for the best in it.
7. **Purpose.** I make sure that I have something in my life that gives me a sense of purpose and makes me feel valuable.

8. **Self care.** I look after my body by eating well and having plenty of exercise. I also try and do something relaxing every day.
9. **Fun.** I spend time having fun and doing stuff that makes me feel happy.

It's quite a long list but don't be put off. I will help you to incorporate all of these kind of things into your action plan in a clear and simple way later in this section.

➤ ***And, remember, it is much harder to change your programming when you are older so you probably won't have to work as hard as me. Your brains are still developing and are more fluid. In fact, some of you might even find that just reading this book is enough to give you a shift in how you see yourself and to make you happier.***

Making a commitment

Since I've started these practices, I've realised that there are two other really important things that you have to do:

1. **You have to really WANT to change.** You have to make a commitment to it, to be really willing. You almost have to reach a place where you just can't carry on any more like you have been, perhaps due to extreme unhappiness or an illness.
2. **You have to let go of the story that there's something wrong with you that needs fixing.** Instead, you need to focus on reconnecting with who you really are. It is important to do some clearing work but all the time you are obsessing over the things that are wrong with you and that need fixing and changing, you are creating more and more stuckness.

So let's make a commitment right now. It's time to feel really excited about life again. It's time to know that there is absolutely NOTHING wrong with you. It's time to blossom into the amazing human being that you were designed to be so that you can feel happy, calm, powerful, confident, loving and positive.

And it's going to be fun and easy!

CHAPTER 2

Creating a great future

Before we look at creating your action plan, we are going to write some life scripts. These will help you understand the impact that your wallpaper is having on your life right now.

More importantly, they will also help you to be clear about how your life could be instead. We need to create a vision for the future otherwise it's easy to get stuck in how things are now.

Life scripts

SCRIPT 1: Your life right now

First we are going to create a script based on how your life is now. Box 15 contains a sample script for a character called Lauren, so read this first.

Then write down the following, using the same format as Lauren's script:

1. How your life is and what you are struggling with
2. How each of these four things are affecting you:
   - Trying to be like everyone else
   - Creating an untrue story about yourself
   - Not loving yourself
   - Unresolved trauma

BOX 15 Sample script 1: Lauren's life now

1. **What am I struggling with**

   I get really anxious all the time. No-one likes me because I am weird and different. I don't fit in and all I want is to be normal like everyone else. I tend to avoid social situations and keep to myself. I have a few friends but I'm not sure how much they like me. Secretly I hate myself. I'm really unhappy with the way I look as my thighs and nose are too big and my hair goes frizzy all the time. And I always argue with my mum. She prefers my brother to me anyway. I'm not very clever, in fact I'm not very good at anything. The only thing I enjoy is eating, particularly chocolate. My life sucks.

2. **How are the four reasons affecting me**
   - **Trying to be like everyone else** Yes this is a big one for me. I really want to be like everyone else and I spend a lot of time focusing on all my faults. 9/10.
   - **Creating an untrue story about myself** Yes I have lots of stories about myself including how I look and how my mum doesn't love me as much as my brother. 8/10.

3. What habits and patterns are holding you back?
4. How do your emotions affect you and how do you deal with them?

SCRIPT 2: Creating an amazing new life

Now let's create a script for how you would like your life to be. This needs to be based on reality – I'm not encouraging you to write a script where you are a world famous pop star with millions of adoring fans and enough money in the bank to buy a whole country! We are going to base it on who you really are, the best version of yourself.

- **Not loving yourself** Again a big one for me. I hate myself. 10/10.
- **Unresolved traumas** I think I'm okay on this one although I do have a small trauma from the time that someone told me I was really weird. 5/10.

3. **What habits and patterns are holding me back**

   I am always focusing on myself and all my problems. I go round and round in my head. I don't eat very healthily and don't have much exercise. I spend a lot of time on social media looking at everyone else's perfect lives. I don't share my problems but tend to hide away in my room. I often come across as unfriendly but really I'm just awkward and shy. I'm not very connected to other people. I give up easily.

4. **How do my emotions affect me and how do I deal with them**

   I hide my emotions from other people and they build up inside me. I often snap or get upset over something small. I don't think it's okay to get angry or to cry in front of people.

Again, I have created a sample script for Lauren, so read Box 16 first. Then write down your answers to these questions:

1. **What is good about your life right now?** Look at every area of your life and write down as many positives as you can find.
2. **What are your unique gifts?** What are you good at? What defines you? Dig deep, ask other people to help you if you find this hard.
3. **Bearing in mind your uniqueness, how would you like to feel right now?** Who would you like to be? What would you like to have? What would you like to do? Create a whole new picture of yourself.

BOX 16 Sample script 2: A new life for Lauren

1. **What's good about my life right now**

   My family care about me, even if we argue sometimes and my brother is annoying. I get on really well with my dad. Our house is great, nice and big and I have my own bedroom. We have plenty of food and I have an iPhone and my own TV in my room. My walk to school is easy and it's a good school. My health is good and I have good skin and I like my hands. Every Saturday I go to a trampolining class which I really love. There are a couple of nice friendly girls there.

2. **What are my unique gifts**

   I am a bit quirky and like to dress in vintage clothes. I am very sensitive so that means I am kind to other people and to animals. I love cooking, especially making cakes and decorating them. I am quite funny when I'm relaxed and love to make people laugh. If I enjoy doing something then I'm really motivated and work hard.

3. **How would I like to be/feel/have/do right now**

   I would like to be able to dress exactly how I want, without worrying about what others think. I'd like to feel really comfortable in my own skin at all times and not to care if I'm a bit different. I'd like to find some friends who really get me. I'd like to feel calmer and not to worry so much. I'd like to bake cakes for friends and earn a bit of money. I'd like to have more fun and more laughter and stop worrying about stupid things like my big nose. I'd like to find a really good way of styling my hair. I'd like to eat more healthily and lose a bit of weight. I'd like to feel happy again like I did when I was young.

Future fantastic

Box 17 contains two future versions of Lauren:

1. How she might end up if she doesn't change her beliefs and perceptions.
2. A brighter version which she can achieve by understanding and liking herself better and by clearing down her wallpaper.

Have a go at creating your own future self script, following the same format as Lauren's script with two future versions. This will help you to see how your life might be if you keep your same old wallpaper, or how it might be if you decide to follow your action plan and make some changes.

When doing the second version, have fun with it. Close your eyes and really connect with how you will feel when you have these things. See yourself living it and feeling really happy and confident. See all the people around you feeling happy that you are happy. How does your body feel when you are seeing all of this? How do you feel in your heart?

➤ ***If you find it difficult to think of anything positive, don't put any pressure on yourself. Just build it up slowly, adding one little thing at a time (as if you are slowly painting a picture). If it's really not flowing then try coming back to it another day when you feel in a more positive mood. You could also ask someone who knows you well to help you with it.***

Once you have created this new picture, bring it into your mind every day, as often as possible. You can do this when you find yourself thinking negative thoughts as it will help distract you. And why not draw the new picture or make a mood board and cut out things from magazines that remind you of this new positive future you.

Remember, the more you focus on it the more your subconscious mind will be taking it on.

BOX 17 Lauren's future self

Version 1 **If I don't make any changes to my wallpaper, this is how I might end up as an adult:**

I am overweight and constantly on diets. I don't have any self discipline so this makes me really down on myself as the diets never work and I hate the way I look. I don't have the confidence to wear nice clothes or makeup. I took the first job that came along and I'm stuck in it as I'm scared to move jobs or ask for a promotion. I feel tired and depressed at the end of the day so never have the energy for any hobbies. I don't have many friends I am not really close to anyone. I have fallen out with my brother and don't see my parents very often. I spend a lot of time alone eating chocolate, watching TV and scrolling through Instagram where I constantly see what amazing lives everyone else has. I often feel lonely and my life feels a bit pointless.

Version 2 **If I can get back in touch with who I really am and let go of all my negative thoughts and beliefs, my life could look like this:**

I love baking cakes. I started off making cakes for friends and friends of my parents and got so busy that I set up my own business. I employ two other girls and we all work well together as a team. I am a little bit overweight but I don't care as I am busy baking cakes and anyway, who wants a skinny baker! I have a lovely boyfriend who is very different to me but it just works. He works with computers and has a geeky mind which I love. I love clothes and have fun with my vintage style. In the evenings I spend time with my boyfriend or my friends. But I am also happy to have a quiet night in watching TV or posting pictures of my cakes on Instagram.

CHAPTER 3

Solutions for change

Throughout the book I have made many suggestions for ways to change your thoughts, feelings and beliefs. Before we start putting together your action plan in the next chapter, I thought it would be useful to list all of these in one place (and I have added a few more).

I have divided them into three sections:

1. **First aid solutions.** Quick fixes for when you are having a bad moment.
2. **Regular practices.** Little things that you can do every day that will help you to change your habits and perceptions.
3. **Deep work.** Ideas to help you get rid of all the deep stuck stuff that is littering up your wallpaper and stopping you from being your true self.

First aid solutions

We all have bad days. If you feel really stuck in negative emotions or negative thinking then try some of the following quick first aid solutions:

- **Distract yourself.** Do something absorbing or something that you love doing. Watch a film, talk to a friend, read a book or do something creative like drawing, painting, writing, cooking, etc.
- **Do a boring job.** As you feel so rubbish, you might as well do something useful. Find the worst possible job – do some homework, tidy your

room, help your mum with something. I bet you will feel better afterwards AND you'll have got a horrible chore out of the way.

- **Have some exercise.** Go for a walk, a run or a swim. Or go to the gym if you have membership.
- **Do the power pose.** This will make you feel more powerful and less overwhelmed by your negative feelings (see Box 5 on page 57).
- **Breathing.** Calm your nervous system with 4-7-8 breathing (see page 133).
- **Have a good cry.** Really let all that emotion come up and out of your body. You will feel much better afterwards.
- **Meditate.** Do a meditation to help calm your thoughts (see page 127 for ideas or check out the Resources page on my website).
- **Mindfulness.** Go for a walk, move around or eat in a really slow and mindful way, engaging with your senses (see page 130).
- **Affirmations.** Say some affirmations or some universal affirmations (see pages 46 and 47).
- **The BAE technique.** If you are experiencing strong emotions, use this technique to allow them to be fully felt (see pages 68-70).
- **The present moment.** See your timeline and notice if you are focusing on the past or on the future. Get into your present moment channel (see page 136).
- **Tapping.** Do some simple tapping on how you are feeling in this moment ("Even though I feel terrible/depressed/angry/sad/worthless").
- **Focus on your senses.** Find five things you can see, four things you can hear, three things you can feel, two things you can smell and one thing you can taste. Repeat this exercise until you feel calmer.
- **Stop fearing the future.** Ask yourself if you are safe right now? Remember, you only ever need to deal with the next ten seconds!
- **Emotional dump.** Take yourself somewhere private and really express how you are feeling. Cry, scream or make any other noises that feel good (you can do it all silently). Allow your body to act out how it wants.

Regular practices

The following is a list of things that are useful to practice regularly so that you can build up some new habits:

- **Tap yourself positive every day.** As soon as you start to feel anything negative, tap until you feel better. Do this as often as you need to.
- **Be kind to yourself.** Watch out for the little voice in your head. What is it saying to you? Treat yourself as your new best friend.
- **Meditate.** Try and meditate every day. There are plenty of meditations online, and you can even get an app that helps you with it. Check out the Resources page on my website.
- **Relax your brain.** Listen to a binaural beats meditation to train your brain to be more relaxed.
- **Practice mindfulness.** This will help you stay more in the present moment. Try it on activities like eating, walking or having a shower.
- **Stand back from your 3D web.** This will help you to observe yourself and to give you better perspective.
- **Get in touch with your true self.** This will help you to get back in touch with a much more powerful and happy part of yourself.
- **Connect with your childhood self.** Draw them, write a poem, create an avatar. See what they want from life. Communicate regularly.
- **Explore spirituality or religion.** This can help you to feel happier.
- **Stop blaming.** Take responsibility for your emotions and feelings. No-one can MAKE you feel anything. They are just triggering your wallpaper.
- **Watch your thoughts.** Notice when you are having fearful and negative thoughts. Just say 'no' and focus on something else. Your conscious mind is like a spotlight and you can choose where to shine it.
- **Give up on perfection.** It's a complete waste of time. Embrace making mistakes and getting things wrong.
- **Be comfortable with failure.** See failure as a stepping stone to achievement. Learn from it and don't give up.

- **Give up the need to be in control.** You will never control your life so relax and allow yourself to flow with whatever comes your way.
- **Step out of your comfort zone.** Practice doing things you find hard or uncomfortable. This will improve your confidence.
- **Choose happiness.** You have to choose to be happy. Focus on something that makes you happy rather than on being negative and miserable.
- **Don't fear the future.** Stop living in an imaginary future, making predictions about how everything is going to be and how you are going to feel. You will probably get it all wrong anyway!
- **The BAE technique.** Practice this as often as possible so you can keep your emotions cleared down (see pages 68-70).
- **Release.** Release pent up emotions regularly. Have a good cry, shout or do it via a physical activity. Find the best way that works for you.
- **Express your emotions.** Experiment with handling them differently. The more you can express them when they arise, the less they will build up.
- **Be in your body.** Be aware of your body and how it feels. Remember it will be giving you feedback about what is going on in your mind! Relaxing the body will also feed back to your mind that all is well.
- **Journalling.** Keep a journal about how you are feeling and write in it every day.
- **Be grateful.** Notice all the things in your life that are good and be really grateful for them.
- **Accept yourself.** Just be okay with yourself right now EXACTLY as you are, even with the things you see as faults.
- **Accept life.** Go with the flow of whatever life brings you. If it brings you something difficult then ask yourself what you can learn from it.
- **Have fun.** Do more of the things that make you happy. Laugh and be silly. Don't take yourself too seriously.
- **Stop caring what others think.** Everyone is stuck in their own heads and stories. No-one really cares what you are thinking, feeling or doing. Just be yourself and stop worrying about how you might be coming across.

- **Be body real.** Stop looking at images of beautiful people and models and look instead at real people in real life. We are all different and that includes how we look.
- **Connecting with others.** Make little friendly connections with people around you – teachers, shop assistants, other teenagers at school, etc.
- **Learn good social media habits.** Unfollow people who don't make you feel good so that you have a positive social media environment.
- **Keep phone safe.** Avoid too much time on your phone and keep it away from your body as much as possible. Turn it off at night.
- **Improve your diet.** Eat less junk food, sugar and sweeteners. Work out what food makes you feel good. Learn to cook.
- **Take supplements.** Magnesium and B vitamins are very helpful for calming the nervous system.
- **Have more exercise.** Join a club or gym, go running, play online fitness programmes, do yoga, walk regularly, etc.
- **Get fresh air and sunshine every day.** Get out in the sun every day and avoid wearing sunscreen.
- **Watch your posture.** What positions are you mainly holding yourself in? Make sure you regularly stretch in the opposite direction.
- **Get plenty of sleep.** Create good sleep patterns by switching off devices and avoiding blue light near bedtime. Try and stick to a routine.

Deep work

The best way to make deep and lasting changes to yourself is to work on getting rid of all the stuck stuff that is littering up your wallpaper, and also to get back in touch with your true self.

Here are some ideas for ongoing deep work:

- **Be yourself.** Really start to understand yourself better so that you can find out who you really are. Notice your gifts. Ask others how they see you (and believe them!).

- **Your story.** Challenge the story you have about yourself. Is it really true? Try and see it with bigger perspective and change it for something that makes you feel more positive.
- **Love yourself.** If you don't really love (or even like) yourself, who made you feel unloveable? What can you do to change it?
- **Traumas.** Are there any traumas that are affecting you? Get help with them if they are very overwhelming or hard to connect with.
- **Building resilience.** If you think you might have developmental trauma or you have a lot of freeze response trauma locked away, get some help so you can make your nervous system more resilient.
- **Limiting beliefs.** Work out which limiting beliefs are affecting you (see Box 1 on page 45 for a list of core limiting beliefs) and start changing them.
- **See what triggers you.** Notice the things and people that regularly affect you and see if you can go behind the reaction to see what is really at the root of your feelings.
- **Strong emotions.** If you often have the same strong emotion, dig down and see what is really behind it. It is hiding a more vulnerable emotion?
- **Repressed emotions.** If you struggle to connect with or express your emotions, look at why this might be. Is this a family pattern? Are you scared to show parts of you? Are you scared of being out of control?
- **Negative emotions.** Make a list of the emotions you struggle with and practice feeling them. See Chapter 4 in the Emotions section on page 77 for why each emotion is useful and what it might be showing you about yourself.
- **Notice resistance.** Be aware of when you are resisting things. What are you regularly resisting and why? What is really behind it?
- **Forgiveness.** Let go of things that others have 'done' to you in the past. It is difficult to feel happy when you are angry with other people. Forgive yourself too if you think you've done something wrong.
- **Draw or map out your 3D web.** This will help you to get some perspective about all the patterns you are stuck in.

- **Your true self.** Try and connect with your true self as much as possible as this will help you to move forward in a more positive way. You can do this through childhood memories, or sitting quietly and connecting.
- **Symptoms as clues.** Read the relevant bits in Section 8 so that you can understand what your mental health symptoms might be showing you about what's going on in your wallpaper.

Future positive

It's good to start focusing on what you DO want rather than all the things you DON'T want. Here are some ideas for positive things for the future:

- **Join a club or start an activity you enjoy.** It's good to get out and spend time with other people. Find something you like doing. You might have to try a few things.
- **Be creative.** Creative things like drawing, painting, writing, sewing, modelling and cooking can help us get more into our right brain. This is very calming and helps us feel peaceful and happy.
- **Visualise.** Create a really clear positive future picture for how your life could be and focus on it as much as possible. Really get in touch with how it feels in your body and your heart.
- **Mood boards.** Create mood boards by cutting things out of magazines that inspire you and remind you of who you really are and how your life could be. Stick these up in your bedroom.
- **Positive EFT.** Regularly do positive EFT on yourself (see page 99) so that you can start to get more in touch with the qualities you feel you lack. This will help you to feel more peaceful, stronger, happier, etc.
- **Spend more time outdoors and in nature.** Get out in nature. Perhaps your garden or a park or some woods.
- **Laugh and more have fun.** Find things that are fun. Perhaps a silly game with your family or something you can do with your friends. Or watch a comedy show. What makes you laugh? Who makes you laugh?
- **See each day as blank canvas.** Don't hold onto the past. Make each day the start of a new and bright future.

- **Do something that scares you.** This is a great way to overcome fear and to make you feel more confident. You can do something really big or just take baby steps towards that thing.
- **Notice what you are focusing on.** What are you giving your attention to throughout the day? Is it making you happy? If not, can you redirect your thoughts and find something more positive to focus on?
- **Focus on loving others.** By changing your filter and seeing everyone in a more loving way, this helps you to practise loving yourself more.
- **Be grateful.** Focus on all the good things that you have in your life. Make a gratitude list every evening, writing down ten things that were good about your day. Look out for things to be grateful for.
- **Get fit and healthy.** Commit to doing regular exercise and improve your diet. Take supplements to calm your nervous system. Being physically strong and healthy will make you feel better mentally.
- **Help others.** It always makes us feel better to help others. Ask your parents if there is anything you can do to help, go and visit a grandparent (call them if they don't live nearby), or ask a friend or neighbour if they need help with anything. You can also find voluntary jobs such as working in a charity shop.

CHAPTER 4

Taking action

So, are you ready to start creating positive mental health?

In this chapter I am going to help you to create a personalised action plan. This plan will help you to work out what things you need to change and will give you a simple structure for making these changes. I have designed it so that it is easy to follow and will fit around your school week.

Some of you won't want to follow a plan and would rather take action in your own way. That's okay. It doesn't really matter what you do but do commit to SOMETHING otherwise you'll be stuck with your poor mental health. There are lots of suggestions for you to follow throughout the book and I have listed them all in the previous chapter.

Five core steps

Whether you want to create an action plan or you want to work in your own way, the following five steps are important for making changes:

1. **Understand.** Get a sense of what your big issues are. What untrue stories, limiting beliefs, unresolved traumas, habits and patterns are holding you back? What issues constantly come up for you again and again? How are they affecting your life?
2. **Notice.** Be aware of how you operate. What you are thinking? What are you feeling? How are you reacting? What triggers you? What you are

saying? How are you interacting with others? What are you putting your attention on? Watch yourself like a hawk.

3. **Clear.** Constantly clear your emotions down by fully feeling and expressing them. This includes repressed emotions that you are holding on to from past events and also ones that arise for you each day. Also clear down any traumas that are affecting you.
4. **Connect.** Keep working on connecting to your true self. The more you can love and accept yourself and see your true power and amazingness, the easier everything else will get.
5. **Create.** Be clear about what you want to create for the future. What do you want to be, have and feel? What new habits can you create? How can you react differently to life? What new things can you try? Who are you and what makes you feel happy?

Preparing a space

Whatever action you decide to take, it is useful to set up a special space for your practices. Your subconscious mind will quickly start to connect this space with your practices and this will help you turn them into a habit.

Many of you will have your own bedroom that you can use. If you have to share your room with a sibling, see if you can get some time alone there every day. Or is there another room you can use (an office or even your parents' bedroom?).

Once you have found a suitable room, choose a cosy corner. Then customise it so that it feels like a good place to sit. Get a chair or a big cushion to sit on, have a blanket so you are warm. Make it feel like somewhere you want to spend time.

➤ ***As well as using this space for your new practices, you can also just go and sit in it if you are feeling really stressed. Your subconscious mind will associate it with feeling calm and safe and so it will make you feel better.***

Creating your action plan

For those of you who would like to create an action plan, let's make a start.

You will need access to the internet and about half an hour of quiet time. If it's not a good moment now then come back to it later.

Then follow these two steps:

1. **Fill in the questionnaire.** Go to www.eleanorhatherley.com/books and click on the green QUESTIONNAIRE button under the *Hello Happy!* book cover.
2. **Fill in the action plan.** Go to www.eleanorhatherley.com/books, and click on the purple ACTION PLAN button under the *Hello Happy!* cover.

For those of you who aren't planning to create an action plan, it would still be useful to fill out the questionnaire. It will help you to be clear about what you need to work on.

Following your action plan

Once your action plan is filled in, follow it for TWO WEEKS. Do it every day. If you miss a day, add a day on to the end so that you still do two weeks.

When you have followed your action plan for two weeks, download another action plan template. Fill it in, choosing the next highest scoring issue from your questionnaire. Also choose a new set of future positive actions, first aid solutions and lifestyle changes. Work with this new plan for another two weeks.

Continue to do this, creating a new action plan for each of the high scoring issues on your questionnaire and working on each one for two weeks. Choose different future positive actions, first aid solutions and lifestyle changes for each action plan.

➤ ***Be as creative as you like with your action plans. You don't need to do them exactly as I've suggested. Find ways of working that suit you.***

Once you have worked on all your big issues, see how you feel. Why not redo the questionnaire to see if the numbers have come down a bit? This will also show you what you still need to work on. You probably won't feel completely better but you might find that things have got slightly easier and that you have had some shifts. You may even feel a little bit more relaxed and happy.

If you really struggle with your mental health, it is a good idea to continue to work on yourself every day. Find a way of working that suits you. Whatever you choose to do, I recommend that you continue with the daily Clear, Connect and Create exercise (see Box 18), or something similar. This will prevent negative thoughts, feelings and emotions from building up and will help you to get back in touch with who you really are.

Staying motivated 

Making self-improvement changes can be really hard work. But it can also be relatively easy. We are all different and there is no right or wrong.

Some people just get to the point in their life when they feel as if they have had enough and are ready to move into a new way of being. They will be aware of their old patterns and will stop themselves going into them. They will take consistent action and will create a better way of being.

Others will find it really difficult to make changes. They will constantly get sucked back into negative thoughts and emotions and will find it hard to stay motivated. They might also believe that they are not worth the effort.

However you experience it, the main thing is just to keep going. Don't create a whole story about how you can't do it, or how it's harder for you than for others. Just keep plodding on. Remember, you are building a whole new house and it's going to take time, so be patient!

Make a pact with yourself that this is a journey, however it looks. It will unfold in exactly the right way for you. You just have to take the first step and make a commitment to doing it. That's all. There will be many backward steps during the process but that's okay as long as you are

BOX 18 Clear, Connect and Create exercise

Start by spending just a few minutes on each part of this exercise. You can then slowly build the time up as you get more practised at it. Sit upright with your eyes closed throughout.

Clear Start by asking yourself how you are feeling. Are you worried about anything? Has something stressful happened that you just can't let go of? Just allow all your feelings and emotions to come up. Really accept them and allow them to expand and fill your body, as in the BAE technique. Let your body do whatever it needs to do to express the feelings – cry, do a silent scream, move around, etc. If anything feels stuck then do some simple tapping and try again ("Even though I feel..., I'm okay").

Connect When you feel calmer, bring your awareness back to the room. Focus on any nearby sounds, giving them your full attention. As you relax, listen out for more distant sounds. Expand your awareness outwards and see if you can get in touch with a sense of space, stillness and peace, where nothing matters and all is exactly as it should be. Sit with this for a few moments. Then see if you can get a sense of connecting with your true self, the self that you really are rather than the one that is stuck in your web. It might take a bit of practice. Sit with whatever comes up.

Create Now think about how you would like to feel. What qualities would you like to experience? Perhaps you want to feel calm, or happy, or powerful, or safe, or loved? Pick a quality and do some positive EFT on yourself (see page 99). If you don't like tapping, just focus on the quality and get a sense of breathing it in, filling your body with it. Really feel the energy of it in your body and imagine you have that quality. Ask yourself what it would enable you to have, feel, be or do. Choose a different quality each time you do this exercise.

generally moving forwards. There are no rules about how fast or slow you do it. You are young and you have plenty of time.

➤ ***Think of your life like a self-improvement game. You can always get a higher score!***

Getting the best from your practices

Here are a few tips for getting the best from your practices:

- If you find it hard to stay motivated, get someone to help you. You could even find a friend who wants to change their life too and you could create actions plans together and connect regularly about your progress.
- Create a routine. If you do the same thing every day at the same time you will create a habit and this will make it easier to stay motivated.
- Keep a journal and write down any major breakthroughs or learnings.
- Don't be hard on yourself if you miss a day. Just continue the next day.
- Remind yourself that this is the start of a long journey and not a quick fix. Give yourself a long-term target such as six months to see any improvements.
- Tap on any resistance to making changes. Find the defective thoughts that are blocking you.
- Get additional help from a professional if you need to. Some issues will be too difficult to clear by yourself.

Keep testing your work. Notice how are you reacting to life and what is going on with your thoughts and emotions. Do you feel happier? Sometimes we don't notice the progress we are making – it's easy to see problems but as it's our natural state to feel relaxed and happy we don't always notice when we are feeling better.

Enjoy reconnecting with the happy you!

CONCLUSION

I hope that you have enjoyed learning about your mental health in more depth and that you will make some changes and reclaim your happiness.

I would encourage you to read other similar books and to explore stuff online. This kind of work is an ongoing journey and it can be helpful to read around the subject as there are many different approaches and ideas.

Check out my website too at www.eleanorhatherley.com. There is lots of useful stuff on there, including:

- **A 40-day online video version of the book.** Each day is based on one chapter and consists of a short video and an exercise to practice. It is ideal for people who don't like reading and is also a good way for those who HAVE read the book to really wire it into their subconscious. There is a lot of information in the book so it doesn't do any harm to revisit it all. The exercises are easier to do too as I will be reading them out loud. Check it out at www.eleanorhatherley.com/video-programmes.
- **Workshops.** If you would like some help with EFT, you can book onto one of my online workshops. You can sign up to get notifications about upcoming events at www.eleanorhatherley.com/sign-up.
- **Useful resources.** You will find links to mental health support organisations, different types of therapy, EFT demos, meditations, books and articles at www.eleanorhatherley.com/resources.

And why not follow me on Instagram and Facebook at @hellohappyteen. I post regular thoughts and tips to keep you inspired and it's a good place to connect with other like-minded teenagers.

This book is WAY longer than I was planning so I'm now going to leave you with one last summary of how to have a really happy life:

- **Have a good relationship with yourself.** Value, love and accept yourself exactly as you are.

- **Have a healthy relationship with your emotions.** Express them freely as they come up and don't repress them.
- **Address any traumas.** Use EFT to work on anything that triggers you or seek some professional help.
- **Don't resist what is.** Be open to whatever life brings you and know that every experience is an opportunity for you to grow.
- **Embrace failure and reject perfectionism.** Failure will help you to improve whereas chasing after perfectionism is very destructive (and, anyway, you are perfect exactly as you are right now!).
- **Look after your body.** Eat healthy food, exercise regularly, sleep well and get fresh air and sunshine.
- **Practice relaxation techniques.** Practice meditation, mindfulness or another relaxation technique every day. This will help to reduce stress.
- **Create an action plan and stick to it no matter what.** Remember that making changes takes time. Just keep going and see it as a journey.
- **Connect with your true self.** This will help you to get back in touch with a happier and more confident you again.
- **Have fun and follow your joy.** What makes you feel alive and happy? Do these things AS MUCH AS POSSIBLE.

And remember, **every single one of you is truly amazing, unique and powerful.** If you don't believe me then that shows there's more work for you to do!

ABOUT ME

I spent the first part of my working life as an editor and graphic designer. But, after my daughter was born, I decided I wanted to do something completely different so I started training as a counsellor.

Around the same time I discovered EFT and used it to clear a trauma that I had had, and also to help control anxiety. I found it very helpful and started using it regularly on myself.

I decided to train as an EFT practitioner so that I could help others. I also continued to attend other therapy-based courses, including Matrix-Reimprinting (an advanced EFT technique for clearing traumas), META-Health (a radical new approach to health) and Human Design.

I am really passionate about helping people to live a happy and healthy life and to get back in touch with the very best version of themselves. Although I enjoy working one-to-one, I wanted to connect with a wider audience and so I started writing this book.

It has had the most amazing flow right from the beginning. Every time I was struggling with something, someone would come along with the exact right information or skill to help me. And because of my publishing background I also found that I had all the skills to put a book together.

I have loved writing it so much that I am now writing one for young adults and am also planning one for adults too. You can check out my progress on my website, www.eleanorhatherley.com.

Printed in Great Britain
by Amazon

62812637R00149